The Wondrous Journey

Into the Depth of Our Being

Ilie Cioara

The Wondrous Journey

Into the Depth of Our Being

BOOKS

Winchester, UK
Washington, USA

First published by O-Books, 2012
O-Books is an imprint of John Hunt Publishing Ltd., Laurel House, Station Approach,
Alresford, Hants, SO24 9JH, UK
office1@o-books.net
www.o-books.com

For distributor details and how to order please visit the 'Ordering' section on our website.

thesilencebook.blogspot.com

ISBN: 978 1 84694 951 7

A CIP catalogue record for this book is available from the British Library.

Translation by Petrica Verdes

Design: Lee Nash

Printed in the UK by CPI Antony Rowe
Printed in the USA by Offset Paperback Mfrs, Inc

CONTENTS

Introduction   1

1. Love   7
2. The Freshness of Life   10
3. Truth is Awake and Active   13
4. The "Psychological Void" between Words and
    Thoughts   16
5. Intuition   19
6. The Book of Life   22
7. The "Ego" Dimension and the "Love" Dimension   26
8. Innocence   32
9. Words   35
10. "Self-knowing" Is Not a Method   37
11. Life – A Journey into the Unknown   40
12. The Path of Liberation   42

Happiness   46

13. Beauty   50
14. The Thinker   53
15. Physical and Psychological Death   56
16. The Flash of the Moment   59
17. Levels of Consciousness   62
18. Abandon Yourself to Life   69
19. Happiness Is Independent Of Age   72
20. In the "Psychological Emptiness" We
    Encounter Reality   74
21. Psychic Pollution   76

22. Immensity   80
23. The Surprise of Liberation   83

The Evolution of Consciousness   89

24. Listening   93
25. The Fulfillment   96
26. Spiritual Powers   98
27. I See Pure Consciousness in Everything
and Everywhere   100
28. Responsibility   102
29. Exposing the "Ego"   105
30. We and the World are "One"   107
31. Religion   110
32. Who Am I Truly?   117
33. Some Live As If in a Dream   119
34. Encountering the Boundless   122
35. Wisdom   124

About the Author   133

Introduction

This book is a message to all individuals interested in discovering the Great Truth; each title represents a certain aspect of the encounter with Life in Its Eternal movement and intrinsic newness and freshness from one moment to another.

The uniqueness of the experience – a direct and personal meeting with the moment – is revealed in each title, and it underlines the practical value of this book. In fact, we describe a new way of encountering Life, completely different from all that humanity has done for thousands and thousands of years and continues to do on the path of spiritual evolution.

Through this novel approach, we invite the reader to combine reading with practice; it is an invitation to know oneself. Without this personal, direct and immediate application, the reader will never attain true understanding, nor the spiritual blessings arising from this ever-renewing discovery.

The words used to describe the phenomenon of "Self-knowing" might sometimes repeat themselves, but the actual experience of integration into the Sublime Truth always ensues spontaneously, as a reality discovered moment by moment.

The wondrous adventure on the never-returning path of spiritual evolution excludes – from the very start – any preconceived ideas about the author or about any of the subjects in this book. Eliminate, therefore, the presence of the author and remain utterly alone, face to face with each title and its significance.

In this manner, the investigation of each life phenomenon described by the author is entirely your personal discovery. In order to successfully explore this state, the only instrument you will need is: an *all-encompassing, lucid, alive, total and completely disinterested Attention*.

The spontaneous effect of Attention is similar to that of the rays of the sun; when we open the windows of a dark room, the light of the sun makes any shade or darkness disappear, even from its most obscure corners.

Thanks to the light of Attention, we effortlessly attain the dissolution of the mechanical reactions of the mind and we melt into the "psychological void". In the peace or passiveness of the mind, a blissful phenomenon occurs: transcendence from the finite world into Boundlessness. In this new state, the "ego" has completely disappeared.

In that wonderful moment we attain a new mind, of universal proportions, moving in a perpetual renewal with each flash of consciousness. Simultaneously, new cerebral cells start to function, enabling us to understand the Uniqueness of Truth, revealed spontaneously in the sparkling flash of the moment.

Here is a test which can tell us whether we have correctly applied the flame of Attention. In that fortunate moment we experience a real state of peace within our whole being and we instantaneously attain the state of "being" or the state of "Pure Consciousness".

The phenomenon of absolute spiritual melting into the Great Whole can be called by several names: inner Aloneness, Enlightenment, Kingdom of Heaven, Nirvana, Creative Divinity or God.

In a state of Superconsciousness, we exist and manifest

ourselves absolutely as Love, Beauty, Kindness and Happiness. All these denominations, frequently encountered in all forms of religious literature, are and will remain only vague attempts to express and define "That which is inexpressible and indefinable".

In fact, words, no matter how beautiful they sound, are not and will never be Reality itself, only a mere description. It is impossible to approach Truth using the knowing mind; nevertheless It can be experienced directly. In order to encounter this Reality we need to go deeper, beyond the meaning of these symbols. Each human being is capable of encountering this Uniqueness, but only under the condition of a direct sacrifice of the "personal self" or the "ego" – a possessive, sectarian and confusing structure.

Dissolving or dissipating the egoic structure – fueled by memory images – is not as difficult as it appears at first glance. The simplicity of the experience, as well as the absence of any goal or purpose, makes this phenomenon appear incredible at first.

Let us approach understanding by starting from an undeniable, logical and obvious observation. On the one hand, there is our mind, always limited by its content and the quality of its memory baggage, manifesting itself in the present moment as a fragmentary, imaginary and subjective entity; on the other hand, there is Infinite Existence, in eternal movement, manifesting itself as newness and surprise each unfolding moment.

Seeing this reality, we ask ourselves: Can the mind encompass and comprehend Infinity?! Of course it cannot, and it will never be able to, for they are two separate dimensions. That which is limited cannot embrace the Limitless!

Confronted with this life problem, what can we do about our mind? Absolutely nothing! Seeing its powerlessness, our mind becomes humble; in the silence that ensues, all intellectual speculation comes to an end effortlessly. The unconditional silence of the mind allows the Unique Reality – existent within each of us, as well as everywhere in the whole Universe – to reveal Itself, by Itself, enabling us to live in perfect harmony with ourselves as well as with the rest of the world.

Therefore, we should never content ourselves with mere intellectual knowledge. Such an understanding is and will always remain only a powerless fragment and never all-encompassing totality. Knowledge can even become detrimental, because the individual gives an even greater importance to his fictitious "personal self", amplifying his conditioning.

In order to clear away any doubts, we must mention that it is impossible to reach the Absolute Truth with the help of: reason, analysis, imagination, prayers, repeating formulas or mantras etc. We cannot discover It through any search, effort or will, by depriving our physical body or by forcefully stopping the constant wandering of the mind.

Each such attempt is initiated and sustained by a prior knowledge. This anticipation, based on an image of a desired achievement, has no tangency with Truth manifesting itself as the Unknown and closely connected to the flash of the moment. The known and the Unknown can never co-exist, in any circumstance. The presence of one categorically excludes the other.

Similarly, no religious faith, philosophical concept, analysis, psychoanalysis or method – no matter how promising – can ever lead us to the threshold of Eternity, for a simple, logical and objective reason: such means of approaching Existence and realizing the Sacred Truth have their source in the known, based on memory residues and stored as images. This informational baggage – the "knowing mind" – can only function egocentrically. Any so-called successes are mere fictitious, deceptive, confusing, temporary effects.

***

Each title or subject in this book provides you – constantly and continuously – with the golden key; by using it correctly and spontaneously, it will open the gate to Paradise or the Kingdom of Heaven, which can be found within ourselves.

Here, in the depth of your being, you will discover Divine Perfection or the Great Love, creating – by Itself – radical transformations and eliminating all the residues accumulated on the surface consciousness, as well as on its deeper layers. In this state, as the "personal self" – a creation of the intellect – has completely disappeared, it is impossible to harm anyone, because that someone is "One" with ourselves.

Here is another modality of integrating our being into the Great Cosmic Energy. Wherever you are: at home with your family, in the street, at work, alone or in the middle of a crowd, ask yourself the following question: Do I function as a "Unity"? Am I one "Whole" - body, mind and spirit - perfectly conscious, "here and now"?

If a thought or an image appears, taking you out of the present moment, attracting you towards the past or the future, you simply become conscious of it using all-encompassing Attention. Simply exposing this apparition makes it spontaneously disappear. Completely free from the past, we encounter the next moment, by being "One" with the movement of the Aliveness.

Be aware, nevertheless, of the cunningness of the "ego"; it will try to introduce a purpose or a goal – in other words:

himself – into the experience of living as a complete being. The same "individual self" – sensing that he is losing his importance – will advise you to rely on teachers from the external world: preachers or masters.

Beware of any such spiritual imposters who deceive you and also take advantage of you materially. If they had truly encountered the Sublime Truth even once, they would have completely detached from any faiths or practical methods that they are trying to impose on you. Detachment from these imaginary experts is definitely easier than detachment from the "personal self".

Do not turn what I am trying to explain here – this simple encounter with oneself – into an ideal, a goal or a purpose to achieve.

Let us always be available to the flow of the Aliveness, a constant surprise from one moment to another. This Aliveness or Divinity always manifests itself as perpetual freshness; therefore, it requires us to come out and welcome it just as fresh.

In order to accomplish this freshness: with the flame of Attention we will simply dissipate the reactions of the mind, for they are nothing but mechanical and confusing apparitions. Their unconditional disappearance transports us into a state of psychological freedom and inner harmony, unfolding moment to moment; our mind is extended into Infinity and it unites us with the all-encompassing movement of Life.

Ilie Cioara

Love

The written or spoken word can never be reality,
Uttering the word "love" will never be true love;
It is a meaningless symbol, for the experience is missing,
Harmonizing all into one perception.

Real love has no motives,
Thinking cannot conceive it, senses cannot perceive it,
It knows no fear, it has no purpose,
It is not an emotional state, nor is it excitement.

Love cannot be cultivated, like a garden flower,
Nurturing its growth;
It cannot be offered as a gift
To the individual trapped in the limited dimension.

Patterns, rules cannot contain it,
It cannot be turned into a prisoner of the past.
Love is present in a climate of freedom,
When obsessive thinking stops its madness.

Love is the movement of an integrated, harmonious being,
Boundless beauty – immense joy,
Absolute kindness and selflessness;
Hatred, egocentrism, falsehood are completely excluded.

Its movement is fullness, never returning,
Completely enveloped by love, the human being becomes
a Universe.
The moment you name it, it immediately disappears,
The whole being is detached from its real movement.

If you try to grasp it, to pin it down, that very moment
it flies away,
For you have become fragmented again.
Love heals and transforms all that is unnatural,
It elevates the individual beyond the worldly dimension.

Only love can transform the ugliness, harmonizing all,
The whole world changes, the savage man evolves,
All wars end and holy peace ensues;
The human being and humankind are healed through love.

Ordinarily, we use the word "Love" much too easily, in a superficial way. In reality, it is only an empty word, lacking any content, meaning or value. This is also the case when we make an emotional confession, with our hand pressed to our heart. Such attempts to demonstrate Love are mere deceptive, meaningless statements.

The ordinary thinking mind, regardless of its motivations, can only experience a relative love. For instance, we love our wife, our children, our parents, our country, our political and religious leader, because they will help us reap certain material or psychological benefits; or we hope that in a foreseeable future they will provide certain satisfactions.

This is, in fact, the so-called love we cultivate ordinarily, in our attempts to experience it as fully as possible. In pursuit of this vision, we create attachments which, by their very nature, completely enslave us. We need to always remain alert, so as not to lose that which we possess – the object of our hopes – and also not to be deceived in our expectations. Our thinking process becomes the fiercest enemy of our peace and health. Worries, fears and sorrow – as emotional shocks – create stress and degrade us psychologically and physically.

Whereas authentic Love – as a true manifested phenomenon – represents the revelation of the Sacred existent within us and the integration of our being into Universality.

It is not and it cannot be created by thinking – trapped in time and defined by its memory residues.

The source of true Love lies in a different dimension; thinking has no access to it, and the human mind, no matter how refined, cannot encompass or comprehend it.

Finally, Love, divine in Its essence, is nothing but the original man, free from the superficial layers that he himself created with the passage of time – the fruit of ignorance and arrogance – so obvious in the man-ego of the present day.

Understanding this truth – not just intellectually – but through a direct encounter with our interfering and outdated surface consciousness, leads us to unconditional silence. The whole structure which sustains the "ego" becomes silent, seeing its powerlessness. In the empty space that ensues, Love appears spontaneously.

From now on, the new man becomes a whole universe, enveloping everything with a simple embrace: people, animals, plants, as well as so-called still life. That which we considered to be close to us, whatever we preferred previously – is now being regarded indiscriminately, on the same level as everything else. There is no distinction between what is "mine" and the rest of the world.

Only such encounters transform us radically, through perpetual purification, creating, through us, favorable conditions for the transformation of the world as a whole.

The Freshness of Life

Everything in the Universe is in constant movement,
What is now – in a flash – is consumed and dies,
The old moment is replaced with the new, appearing
                                        rhythmically,
A constant succession – inviting us to know ourselves.

Yesterday and the thousands of yesterdays
Created our lives of fiction: lies, fear, madness;
All that was – is dead – worthless in the present,
The moment – a precious mystery – integrates us
                                        into reality.

We owe everything to the moment,
It offers us all, when we encounter it directly,
Asking for nothing in return, no effort or struggle;
All of our Happiness comes from this simple encounter.

Our whole being is open, in humbleness,
Nothing is anticipated, thinking is completely silent.
There are no expectations, no ideal or purpose to
                                            accomplish,
It is simple: we encounter Life in the content of the
                                            moment.

Spontaneously we detach, nothing is accumulated!
We do not add any values to our small "self";
Our Attention is directed to the new moment, with the
                                            same intensity
We need to give it all our respect and loyalty.

Therefore, moment to moment, Life is always fresh, active,
Showing us how naive we are,
When we believe in faiths and moral systems,
Based on dead things and personal thinking.

The newness, freshness of Life in its unfoldment
Requires us to be the same way – a Sacred Integration;
Repetition is a trap, holding us prisoners,
As "egos", we create our own bondage.

Only by encountering Life in Its unlimitedness
Will we discover Love in the Great Boundlessness;
It dissolves all: pain, torture and sorrow,
Disdain, hate and vanity – the whole conditioning.

All that exists in the immensity of the Universe is in a state of permanent movement and freshness from one moment to another. Each moment appears as a spark, ends its course in a flash and disappears, leaving the path open for the next moment. This way of life requires us to know ourselves as we truly are and not as we would like to be.

Yesterday and the thousands of yesterdays experienced in this life, as well as in countless past lives, have created a deficient structure, in which egotism directs and leads all of our actions. Everything we have lived and experienced in the past exists as mere outdated recordings, old and worthless in the present. These residues prevent us from encountering the mystery of the moment, integrating our being and enabling us to experience Eternity.

Therefore, in whatever circumstances we find ourselves, we must always encounter the eternal newness which the Aliveness in its eternal mobility brings forth. This experience does not require any effort, struggle or sacrifices.

Happiness – to which each living being aspires – can be experienced only in the simplicity of this encounter with Life. Let us, therefore, open our whole being to Life, with a humble attitude, without pursuing any purpose or gain. The mind is completely silent; without expecting anything in return, it directly encounters the mysterious content of Life, unfolding in the moment. Immediately afterwards, we detach, without accumulating anything; with the same intensity, accompanied by lucid Attention, we encounter the next moment, by giving it the respect it deserves. It is only in this constant movement and renewing freshness that we are able to truly encounter Life and understand its meaning.

From the same experience, we also discover how naive and powerless our personal mind is when it relies on faiths, philosophical concepts, moral systems as well as any outdated recordings of the conditioned mind.

Practice can prove to us, beyond any doubt, that the repetition of what we know or imagine is a real trap, holding us prisoners in the dark prison of our small-minded "ego". Only as free beings can we experience the integrity of our being and transcend from the finite world into Boundlessness. In this circumstance, the "personal self" or the "ego" (the personality) disappears by itself – as well as its entire content based on ambition, greed, disdain, fear, pride, sorrow, violence and hatred – in one word, the whole time-space vanity.

Truth is Awake and Active

Truth is eternally awake and in perpetual movement,
Active each moment, in constant renewal.
We have wrongly divided it, creating small or great truths,
Truth is revealed as unity, when we are "psychological
                                        emptiness".

The conditioned mind cannot encounter It,
For it is always confined by its limited nature.
Truth is immense – boundless – Infinite Energy,
Two separate states, different in their essence.

In its powerlessness, the mind must become silent,
There is no other way to detach from the past.
When the limited is silent, the being is extended into
Infinity,
In that moment, the Sacred Truth envelops us instantly.

Present in all and everything, it is within us as well as
within everyone,
It is waiting, day and night, for us to discover it, through
integration.
Do not waste any time! Give yourself to Truth!
Humbleness is the path! Otherwise you keep deceiving
yourselves.

You cannot desire it, search for it, there are no expectations,
This simple encounter with ourselves leads to realization.
Truth is constant freshness, it reveals the Great Happiness,
Free from motivations, independent from thought.

The Absolute Truth – unique source of the whole of
existence – is, through Itself, Pure Reality, alive and active,
in continuous movement. Its simple presence creates
renewing transformations in all the existential forms in the
world of matter, on the perpetually ascending journey of
evolution. Everything that exists today in the Boundless

Universe originates from Truth; and to Truth we shall return, after exhausting the long process of experiences in the world of matter.

Because of misunderstanding, the human being has brought down this One Truth to the level of the mind. With this unfortunate event, the Oneness of Truth has been divided, according to each individual's limited and subjective mind. The chaos, violence, greed, ambition, hatred and arrogance – existent in the world of today – are natural effects of this attempt to bring the Infinite to the level of understanding of the human mind.

If all these statements are very clear, not because anyone said so, but evident through themselves and their obvious effects, we ask ourselves the question: What is the solution? What can we do about it?

There is only one solution, namely: to renounce the error that our ancestors made – in this very moment.

The human mind – conditioned by time and space – is and will always remain limited, no matter how erudite it may be. Therefore, it will never, in any circumstance, be able to encompass and comprehend the Absolute Truth.

The Infinite, nevertheless, has the perfect capacity to encounter the finite, limited world, confined by itself.

In order to avoid any ambiguity, we must emphasize that this phenomenon cannot occur the other way around. The finite is and will always remain incapable of understanding the Sublime Truth.

Only when the mind is silent, in humbleness, for it has understood its powerlessness, in that moment of inner aloneness, the Supreme Truth, existent in the depths of our being, is revealed in all Its splendor and beauty.

In fact, this is the true purpose of the descent into the current incarnation, in the ephemeral climate of earthly existence. Let us, therefore, not waste time with trivial and deceptive occupations.

The very fact that we are reading these words, in this moment, is a true sign that we have reached a sufficient level of spiritual maturity enabling us to realize the great mystery.

We cannot search for the Absolute Truth; we cannot desire It, nor can we discover It through expectations, as a result of mental activity.

Truth is revealed spontaneously, when the "ego" is dissipated under the rays of all-encompassing, lucid and impersonal Attention and our being is integrated. The constant freshness of Truth provides us with boundless Happiness, on moments of existence, free from any worldly motivations.

The "Psychological Void" between Words and Thoughts

In the pause between two spoken words,
Created by reason,
Lies the "emptiness",
A direct encounter.

When words are rare
You encounter this gap;
Connected words
Create the thought process.

The "psychological void" between thoughts
Is beyond meaning;
A silent meeting,
Through total melting.

In this state
There is true comprehension;
This space expands,
Defined by Light.

In "emptiness", the Sacred affirms itself,
The "ego" is shattered;
In this moment
A new man appears – a creative being.

In humble simplicity,
Through "emptiness" we become Eternity;
A natural fulfillment,
Uniting us with the Whole.

The "psychological void", passiveness of the mind or peace of the soul I mention in each topic represents a true window to Infinity. Through this crack in the ego – ensuing naturally – the true nature of our being is revealed as Perfection or Divinity. This divine Reality lies within each human being, without any exception.

During a conversation or a discussion, no matter how fast we speak, we discover that between two words there are small gaps in which thinking is completely absent. These gaps become even more evident when we talk more slowly, consciously creating distances between words.

In these gaps, the "ego" disappears completely and Eternity – existent within us as well as everywhere in the sphere of existence – unites us with the Great Whole; on the other hand, the Light of this Reality makes it possible to rationally connect and understand these words. Therefore, in this "psychological void", the "I" disappears and, in the empty space, the real being expands into Infinity. Thus we discover – through a direct experience – that we are a divine Particle, defining itself as Love and Intelligence in perpetual movement.

The same phenomenon occurs during silent speech, when we do not externalize what we think or imagine. Thinking and imagination are also expressed, in fact, with the help of words.

This space can be extended by simply becoming conscious of it with a lucid, all-encompassing Attention. Let us remind that this Attention is the Sacred itself, manifest in the depth of our being. It makes all nebulous shades of the chaotic activity of the "self" disappear.

In order to avoid any confusion, we need to point out that any efforts of will or imagination are unable to accomplish the "psychological void" we mention in all the poems. This inactivity of the knowing mind is attained without any previous programming, goal or ideal to accomplish. Simply encountering the movement of the mind with the light of lucid Attention creates a state of silence. All the benedictions arise from this silence, and our being is integrated and united with Divinity.

Intuition

Intuition is a surprise – perfect purity,
In a flash we perceive the obvious Reality;
Reality reflects itself in the mirror of our consciousness,
The comprehension envelops our whole being.

The evident mystery has no support in the thinking
                                                    process,
It is revealed through itself, by itself, without any
                                                preparation;
Spontaneously and directly, it opens up
Experiences beyond time – revealing certainties.

Intuition cannot be encountered by searching,
It cannot be cultivated by the mind, through desire and
                                                    effort;
In order to create a climate for this wonderful achievement,
Peace and silence are the secret of attaining this state.

The only obstacle is the "ego" and its residues,
Barging into the present, distorting perception;
The old can never encounter what is real:
Perpetual freshness unfolding in the present.

If we see it as it is – as a dysfunctional obstacle,
Exposing it each moment, it disappears; watching
dissolves it.
Each time the old appears, we encompass it, attentively,
Free from any prejudice or ideals.

This simple meeting pierces it, dissipating it at once,
"Psychological emptiness" ensues, in communion with
silence,
On Its screen of light, manifesting itself as a Reality;
Intuition is a witness to this realization.

We use words only in order to communicate,
To explain the phenomenon of integration,
We can only anticipate further indescribable experiences,
Revealing themselves in a state of aloneness.

Intuition is that capacity of the Divinity of our being to
warn or to direct us in a perfect way through lightning-like
impulses. It is a surprise and an instant mystery. It has no
connection with the conditioned mind. On the contrary, it
reveals itself to us only in the absence of thinking. We can
never, in any way, anticipate its appearance. It cannot be
cultivated and we cannot invoke it with the help of a
certain formula.

Our only duty is to create a favorable climate in which
Intuition can reveal itself, by itself. The only obstacle,
obstructing its mysterious presence, is the "ego" and its
whole memory baggage – a fictitious entity. When we see it
as it is – with the help of lucid Attention – the "ego" disappears spontaneously.

"Psychological emptiness" ensues naturally; our whole being, in perfect harmony and inner simplicity, transcends from the finite world into Boundlessness.

In a state of "Pure Consciousness", intuitive responses are mirrored onto the luminous screen of consciousness. We can explain this state in the right words only when we are requested to do so, in order to provide a better understanding of life phenomena.

These intuitive impulses can reveal to us: either momentary dangers, threatening our lives, or hidden, concealed truths, or small realizations regarding our everyday existence.

Happy indeed is the man who, detached from the "self", abandons himself to the will of Divinity, offering himself as an instrument through which the Divine affirms Its Sacred guidance.

It is only on this level of existence that the human being encounters and experiences true security, something that each inhabitant of planet Earth is continuously searching for.

The Book of Life

Throw away all your so-called holy books,
Throw away your hollow faiths – fruits of a desperate
mind;
Break free from any moral systems
Created arbitrarily by social convention.

If you happen to follow any goals, any models, any ideals
Destroy them from the very start.
This path is based on deceit and conflict,
Thus you become a prisoner of time and its dual fiction.

Instantly empty the vessel of your consciousness
Of all the accumulated past residues;
Completely shatter the past, become free psychologically,
Be one with the present, as an integrated whole.

Thus you can understand, in a real way,
Everything that life brings, with its intrinsic laws.
The book of life lies before you in its infinite dimensions,
Do not be afraid, do not hesitate, dare to encounter it
directly!

It never repeats itself and it has no end,
This book started to be printed from its very mysterious
                                        beginning.
It cannot be read through interpretation,
For the old understanding distorts its perception.

Completely silent, we just watch each event as it appears
And quickly, we stay open to the incoming moment,
Persistent observation and attentive listening
Integrate our being and provide full understanding.

If we miss a moment, while listening and watching,
We become isolated from the new and lose integration.
Thus the thread breaks, we lose ourselves in the past.
Reading the Book of Life – we need to move in syntony
                                        with the moment;

It requests of us a total attention,
In order to be available to all that moves in the present,
As well as a perfect, spontaneous contact,
A quick, sharp mind, detached from the known.

Life itself and the act of reading are one movement,
One with the Infinite – a perfect communion.
Do not despair, in the beginning reading is intermittent
                                        and rare,
With much persistence and work, Sacredness will reveal
                                        itself.

More and more integrated – be attentive – for the old man
Appears as a shadow, and with its swift force
It throws you brutally into the past. Persistently expose it,
Each time it appears, encounter it with the flame of
                                                    Attention.

This spontaneous, clear, sharp, all-encompassing
                                        encounter
Dissolves it mysteriously – the new – the integrated being
Moves in timelessness, as immensity, with simplicity,
This is what the Book of Life requests of us: to live in
                                                    reality.

If you truly desire – with all your being – to come into
direct contact with Life as it reveals itself from one moment
to another, we will explain the verse in more detail.

The movement of Life – in the pages of Its book –
manifests itself, by its very nature, as freshness and
absolute newness each passing moment. In order to read
this book and truly understand it, we need to approach it
with the right attitude. We can only encounter the aliveness
in eternal movement with a clear – perfectly lucid –
innocent mind, uncontaminated by any influences or
memory residues of the past.

As a consequence, imposed by the very essence of the
aliveness, we need to eliminate all the knowledge we have
borrowed from various books and recorded in our memory.
No book, regardless of its nature, can direct us towards an
authentic encounter with Life. This is also true even in the
case of authors who undeniably realized the encounter
with the Absolute Truth.

By trying to live according to the teachings described in

these books, we will lead an imitative life, devoid of authenticity. But, as human beings, we have long ago surpassed the stage of development and evolution characteristic of primates.

Therefore, completely detached from the memory baggage, we have a completely free mind, able to encounter everything the mobility of life brings forth.

Besides this openness and availability – the mind in a state of perfect equilibrium – we also notice that there are no expectations of a mysterious result coming from the depth of our being. Completely silent, we just listen and watch each concrete fact brought forth by this perpetual movement.

There are no inner comments, no interpretations, assessments, condemnations or acceptance. We do not draw any conclusions, because in that moment, our mind, completely detached from the past, has a pure energy, able to encompass the Truth in its integrity, providing complete understanding.

The detachment from the experienced moment occurs instantaneously; without accumulating anything from this encounter, we encounter the next moment just as new. In that moment, our being – body and mind – is a single Unity, in perfect union with the Great Cosmic Energy. The Sacred within us, through flashes of consciousness, manifests itself as: Love, Beauty, Kindness and Intelligence.

Reading this book, our being and Life are one single movement, integrated into the Absolute Truth.

By encountering the old, conditioned man with the flame of Attention, the conditioning is annulled and inner harmony ensues; the oneness of being and its integration into the Infinite become one single movement with the act of reading the Book of Life; absolute understanding appears in a state of utter simplicity.

In the beginning, this simple way of encountering life is very difficult to attain. The chaotic mind is the cause of this difficulty; it brutally barges into the present and psychologically throws us into the dark mire of a more or less distant past. The mechanicalness of the thinking process creates the structure of the "ego"; as its authority is endangered, it becomes more aggressive and incisive.

The fiction of the "ego" can be vanquished, to its total annihilation; through a direct, spontaneous and simple encounter with the impulses of all-encompassing Attention, all anachronic reactions are dissipated.

As the "ego" disappears, the "psychological void" opens the gate to Infinity; in a state of happiness, we melt with It.

It is only in this state that the new man, as an intelligent being, living outside time, can create a different world, free from tension, hate, fear and sorrow.

This is the message that the mirror-poem "The Book of Life" invites you to put into practice, in order to truly live an authentic life, in the real sense of the word.

The "Ego" Dimension and the "Love" Dimension

They are worlds apart, different in their essence and
content,

They have nothing in common;
When one is missing, the other is present,
The separation is total, each is independent.

The world of the "ego", the "I" or the "self"
Is limited and old, never freshness;
It has accumulated knowledge and ideas,
Imaginary experiences and facts are its nature.

Here, the whole past of humanity is written,
Humankind's past efforts in the process of evolution;
It is a constant struggle – desires, ideals
In perpetual battle, war after war.

There is no sun and no light,
Only darkness, turmoil, fear, desperation and murder;
Violence and hatred are the emperors,
Arrogance and pride – their trusted advisors.

The world of the fragmented man –
Prisoner of his past, overwhelmed by struggle and
noise –
Has become mechanical, through constant repetition,
Mere conformism, programmed by old ideas.

Whereas the world of Love is called: Truth – Intelligence,
God – Reality – Absolute existence,
In its dimension you encounter true kindness,
Real peace, real serenity, true action.

You cannot describe this sublime world in words,
There are no faiths or ideals – only spontaneous
                                        comprehension;
Living in this dimension, you move free from any baggage,
If you try to put it into words, your happiness disappears.

It is a wondrous realm, here you become restfulness,
Your being is liberated, your energy is utter relaxation.
Conscious and superlucid – you don't know who you are –
Except Quietude-Immensity, in total melting.

In the "ego" dimension, knowledge is valuable,
It teaches and directs you – limited in space and time;
You cannot enter the Infinite World through knowledge,
For it is just an obstacle – any such attempt is absurd.

When, totally attentive, you see your "ego" in action
It is spontaneously dissipated, free from desires;
This is the supreme Moment when we enter Infinity,
Beyond any doubts, we become one with the Sublime.

The human being, the most evolved life form on this planet, has two distinct levels of existence. Ordinarily, man functions in the dimension of the "ego"; egocentrism is his intrinsic characteristic, directly influenced by this level of existence and expression. In fortunate, exceptional cases, when he manages to detach from this plane, he encounters a new dimension, called "Love", pure Energy or the Infinite.

The two dimensions have nothing in common; they are

completely separate. Neither one is the source or the continuation of the other. They cannot co-exist, for they have nothing in common; nothing can unite them. On the contrary, they completely exclude each other. When one dimension is present, the other dimension is completely absent. Each is exclusively independent from the other. The first one, no matter how vast the realm of its knowledge, remains nevertheless limited. The second one is limitless, infinite.

The "I" dimension is also called: ego, self, surface consciousness, personality or the finite world of the individual. It is defined by its very content. On its surface, the whole heritage of the human race is recorded, as well as the legacy of our personal efforts in this existence, as well as in past lives. Experiences, facts, adventures, ideas, faiths as well as various ideals are stored in its content.

In this limited space, a permanent struggle takes place between different desires, as each aspires to supremacy. As soon as one becomes dominant, other desires try to undermine it and take its place.

In the sphere of the "ego", always limited and confined by its shell, there is no light. There is no possibility of light, as long as its fierce desires fight one another for dominance. Ceaseless battles create an atmosphere of confusion, darkness and frequent conflictual states. Violence, its toughest instrument of affirmation, reigns on the highest level, considered to be the most effective weapon, used to achieve all kinds of goals. Hypocrisy often helps violence in its battle strategy, and arrogance enhances its self-importance each time a cheap victory is achieved.

Functioning on this plane, the individual is in a state of constant restlessness; struggle and agitation are the very fabric of his unnatural life. Because of erroneous education, man functions as an automatic mechanism, repeating itself obsessively. By conforming to the educational patterns provided by society, he is unable to come into direct contact with and really comprehend the simple unfoldment of true life.

Any activity we pursue in this dimension, with the purpose of improving or transforming our being, is similar to Sisyphus's efforts. No matter how much water he pours into the barrel of the Danaids, it will always remain empty. Any effort performed by the "self" naturally leads to its enforcement. It might, eventually, enlarge the content of the "ego", through other accumulations, but it will never be able to radically change it. Superficial changes are possible; nevertheless, through them, an even greater illusion is created, for the "ego" is even better camouflaged.

**

The Love dimension is also known by different names: Truth, Reality, God, Immensity, the Infinite, Intelligence etc. The very meaning of the words which define it express the fact that this dimension has no bounds.

In this dimension, no faiths, ideals, desires or any such similar ideas can exist, as they are encountered in the limited dimension. For this reason, in this wondrous climate there is no struggle, contradictions, confusion, pain, hate etc.

Boundlessness cannot be comprehended by imagination or by thought; there is nothing we can say about it. We can only describe and explain that which our mind can encompass. In the face of Limitlessness, the mind is poor, completely unable to understand it. In fact, the moment Immensity affirms itself within us, as a living state of the integral human being, the "ego" dimension and its limited way of expression does not exist anymore.

If, in the span of the moment, the human being – in a state of happiness, melting with Boundlessness – tries to explain this state, he is immediately detached from this dimension and becomes an ordinary person. The intervention of thought and its assessments and knowledgeable conclusions have caused the fall from one dimension to the other.

There is not much we can say about the experience of living in the dimension of Love. Nevertheless, we will try to express certain feelings and states of being encountered in this state.

In complete union with Love, we are perfect peace, we live total freedom; the very notion of "self" is missing, although we are endowed with a clarity and sensitivity of the mind such as we have never encountered in the limited realm of thinking.

By melting with silence, we become that silence, equilibrium and harmony, free from duality: our being is extended into Infinity. Practically, by experiencing "psychological nothingness", the "ego" disappears and, in its place, Immensity envelops us wholly and we become one with It. Integrated into the Great Cosmic Energy, we continue to exist as a state of superconsciousness.

This state of universality and the evolution of knowledge and science have nothing in common. On the contrary, any interference from the knowing mind is a real impediment, preventing us from entering this dimension.

Only a true experience of and within this Immensity operates a radical transformation in the structure of the individual. That and nothing else! Understanding this reality, by ourselves and through ourselves, is truly valuable and significant on the path of spiritual evolution.

How can we realize this state?

Each time, we start by observing the reality of things

and facts directly. First of all, we watch the movement of thinking as a reaction to the encounter with the movement of life. Watching our reactions as we welcome the newness of existence will effortlessly and inevitably lead to their dissolution. The moment of complete silence attained in this manner represents the gate of transcendence into the infinite dimension.

Thinking is completely silent; the state of inner harmony within us shatters the walls surrounding the "ego": free from the limited dimension, we expand into Infinity. The quiet joy we experience in this realm, beyond any motives or reasons, is a clear sign of our integration into this dimension. Only here will we encounter certainty, as well as absolute Truth. Any illusions or deceitful states are completely dissipated.

Innocence

Indescribable beauty, equilibrium and harmony,
Pure clarity, reflected in joy.
When thinking stops and the whole past is dead,
Innocence blooms effortlessly.

It is a complete detachment from everything worldly,
It creates a perfect order, as a natural effect.
Dissolving the "ego", we become Immensity,
Perpetually innocent, we live holy freedom.

Innocence is always new, just like the eternal movement,
It is as fresh as dew, awakening us;
When we are attentive, when we simply observe
The warmongering aggressive "ego", innocence ensues.

Melting in the now – in a direct relationship with
"what is",
We are always innocent, in the incoming moment,
Nothing is accumulated from the fleeting moment,
We are pure action, detached from the known.

The word "Innocence" is relatively easy to understand, semantically and intellectually. Anyone can do it, by simply opening a dictionary.

In this poem, we do not simply refer to such superficial and relative understanding, questionable by its very nature. This is completely different.

Understanding the phenomenon of innocence appears through experience. In this state, innocence itself reveals its mysteries to the human being who encounters it in a real, direct way. Therefore, only the person who becomes one with innocence can describe its characteristics and express them in ordinary words.

Innocence is a quality of the Sacred; it has no connection with thinking – an emanation of the "ego". If thinking, in its vanity, attempts to cultivate innocence, it will only accomplish a caricature of it. As such, Innocence appears only in the definitive absence of the activity of the mind, of the thinking process and the "ego" in all its forms and manifestations.

When Innocence appears, it is always followed by harmony, beauty, purity and joy. It fuels itself through itself, like a burning flame, with an inner combustion. As absolute newness from one moment to another, it is in perfect harmony with Life's universal law of movement.

It is only in this circumstance, through a direct relationship with the reality of things, that we are able to come into contact with the phenomenon of innocence, unfolding here and now.

A natural question ensues: How can we encounter Innocence? Is it necessary to do something, psychologically, or does it reveal itself, by itself, when we create a favorable climate?

As long as we move and act led by the thinking of the ego, we will never know true Innocence. We cannot project its image as an ideal to accomplish through effort or a certain activity of the mind, or any other such attempts.

If this is the way things are – easy to verify through experience – the problem we need to solve is the silence of the ego, without attempting to cultivate or conquer Innocence.

As soon as we reach this level of understanding, the ordinary mind – seeing that its powerlessness has been exposed – becomes completely silent. In this void of activity, a crack opens in the structure of the human personality. It represents a true window, through which the world of the Sacred radiates and enters, enveloping our whole being.

In that happy moment, psychologically, we are outside time and space, integrated into universality. From now on, our whole activity is led by innocence, Love, beauty and joy; we are one with "what is", one with whatever the incessant flow of life brings in its natural unfoldment.

Words

The written or spoken word is nothing but a symbol,
An instrument of expression, sometimes used to praise,
Sometimes to denigrate – according to the tendency
Of the "ego", in its quest for realization.

The human being, in his pilgrimage throughout the
                                                centuries,
Endowed the word with different senses and meanings.
The word is just an echo, a vibration,
Its meaning is never new, but always a repetition.

It creates hopes, worries, imaginary impulses,
There is an obvious distance between concept and
                                                "what is";
The word is never the fact, it is never reality.
The thought and the spoken word create duality.

Words are meaningless, they create conflict,
Different interpretations in constant disagreement;
When we are hungry, we cannot feed ourselves with
                                    the word "bread",
But only with the reality of it, as a concrete experience.

Words and speech separate us from what is real,
They overshadow the being and confuse the mind.
When the mind is wise, it ends all turmoil,
In stillness, inner conversation ceases.

In this humble encounter, we find the source of the
                                                    Sacred,
Thinking is spontaneously silent, revealing the Truth.
By itself and through itself, it detaches us from the
                                                    dimension of time:
In silence, in true peace lies the whole mystery!

In our relationships with the world, with our fellow human beings, with life in all its forms of manifestation, we use words in order to understand each other and to communicate verbally and mentally; they are mere instruments of expression.

These means of expression are nothing but symbols, chosen by the community and used in everyday communication. They have a certain meaning and they describe a thing or a fact; its significance is generally accepted. They have a distinct pronunciation; uttering or just imagining a word can trigger certain sentiments and feelings.

No matter how broad their sense, words can never encompass the essence of a thing in itself, its concrete reality. The word "bread", for instance, does not express the reality of bread. No matter how many times we say this word, it can never satisfy our hunger. We can only satisfy hunger through a direct contact with bread, by eating it.

The same happens in the case of other words, such as: Love, Truth, God. They are nothing but a mere expression and not the reality, the essence of these experiences.

Therefore, in these three examples, we must overcome the narrow limits of the words in order to encounter the actual reality of Love, Truth, God. From this very inquiry, we learn that words prevent us from being united with the reality they are trying to express.

In light of this revelation, the mind, seeing its incompetence, becomes silent by itself, in humbleness, without any intervention on our part.

It is only when thinking completely ceases any activity, when it stops expressing itself in any way, internally or externally, that favorable conditions are created for us to come into direct contact with the reality expressed by the three symbols mentioned earlier.

In other words, by dissolving the "ego", our being – attentive and lucid – is integrated into Universality and directly experiences the state of divinity, manifested as Love and absolute Truth.

"Self-knowing" Is Not a Method

"Knowing" is not a method, a path to accomplishment.
We don't set out with a purpose or an imaginary goal;
Will and effort are meaningless,
All these are connected to the old past.

When there is a method, the "ego" is also present
In each activity – it is never independent;
It always repeats, imitates old patterns – outdated in the
                                                    now,
Constantly pursuing its hideous self-importance.

By applying a method, the "ego" is fortified,
Conditioning is strengthened, inner chaos grows.
We ourselves set the trap and become its victims,
This is what happens when we pursue our "self".

In "Self-knowing", we start only from facts,
All that appears in the moment – true realities;
We are in direct psychological contact with Life,
Just a simple meeting, without any goals or ideals.

We don't pursue anything, not even transformation,
We don't reject "what is", in the moment;
The "ego" is completely excluded from this encounter,
"Psychological emptiness" is the whole secret – immensely
                                                    valuable.

Everything we encounter: thoughts, fears, feelings,
Nagging desires, old obsessive images
Are suddenly transformed and dissipated;
The wondrous meeting can be recognized by its results.

Thus, the Sacred within us reveals itself,
Affirming itself through Love – absolute purity.
There is no other path to realization,
Without this encounter with "Nothingness".

"Self-knowing" is not a religious belief, nor is it a method, because we do not anticipate any ideals to reach, nor set out with a goal in mind, by doing or not doing something. Will, effort, imagination, faith, repeating formulas or mental analysis are unnecessary, for the simple reason that all these are connected to the past and, therefore, they are part of the "ego". This imaginary structure can only repeat old facts, increasing its "self-importance".

Any method, no matter how promising, can only fortify the structure of the "ego", further increasing the chaos within the individual. Functioning on this level, we ourselves set the traps and we fall into them. The reality of these facts demonstrates, beyond any doubt, that we are the victims of our own "ego".

In practicing "Self-knowing", we start only from "what is" – from the reality of facts appearing before us each moment, in the unfolding movement of the Aliveness. We need not do anything other than to come into direct contact with all these apparitions: thoughts, emotional states, desires, images etc. It is just a simple meeting, without pursuing any results or expectations.

The simplicity of the encounter with the movements of the "ego" leads to their disappearance. Both the encounter and the spontaneous disappearance of the reactions of the mind confirm the reality of "Knowing". In this emptiness, we are a simple state of "being" or "Pure Consciousness".

Only in this perfect meeting does a new perspective

open; the Sacred within us manifests itself as Love, Intelligence and absolute Purity.

We can search the whole world, as well as everything that the human mind has imagined or invented, but we will never find anything comparable to the efficiency of this simple encounter, as a state of "Nothingness" or "Psychological Zero".

The "emptiness" or passiveness of the mind – provided by lucid Attention – is an abyss, in which the old, egocentric, arrogant, fearful man disappears. Simultaneously with his disappearance, the true nature of our being is revealed – without beginning or end, in its essence immortal Divinity. This is the new man, destined to create a different world, in which Love and its hallowing impulses is present everywhere, creating a true Paradise on our planet.

Life – A Journey into the Unknown

Life is eternal movement, renewing freshness
From one moment to another – never repeating itself.
Are we truly present to this encounter?
Only by melting with Life can we discover true life!

This journey takes place at an incredible speed,
There is no time to analyze or accumulate anything;
A new brain, a new mind – in permanent flow,
Through flashes of light they are one with the eternal
                                                    present.

Thoughts or expectations are completely excluded,
If we give them time and energy, we fall behind,
The constant contact with the eternal freshness is
                                                interupted
And we miss the moment, the inaction is hollow.

Only through a direct contact do we become an integral
                                                    being,
Spirit, mind and body – an all-encompassing unity.
There are no expectations, nothing to be pursued,
Simple presence is like a mirror, reflecting eternally.

What is Life – Existence in Its unfoldment?
It is Divinity itself, perpetually creative,
A Unique Reality, limitless Eternity in the Immense
                                            Boundlessness,
Present in all and everything – therefore we are also
                                                a part of It!

By searching outside, we stray from the path,
This approach is deceptive from the very beginning!
By worshipping people, holy places and objects,
We neglect the essential – the Sublime Unity and Its
                                                sacredness.

It has always been within us and we can encounter It only
                                                                in one way:
By watching the movement of the mind, in a state of
                                                        attention;
It is a simple encounter, there is no purpose, no
                                                expectations,
In this circumstance, hallowing peace is revealed.

The mind and the heart are humble – the being is
                                        Pure Energy,
We are the Sacred Energy manifested as Love and
                                                Harmony;
A blissful transcendence from the world of knowledge
Unites us with Infinity, as one single movement!

The Path of Liberation

The active, tenacious man, determined to realize his
                                                    potential,
To fulfill his evolutionary destiny, to arrive
Beyond the hideous "self" into the Sublime Infinite;
He is like a fire, a constant flame – a tireless athlete.

Practicing day and night, unhindered, yet without
                                        struggle,
Without "yesterday" or "tomorrow", free from
                                imagination,
He chooses the right path – the path of liberation;
He does not expect transformation to come from the
                                        outside.

In total simplicity, a spontaneous contact,
Free from duality, without any models,
He encounters the present as Life bestows it,
Without hope and without turmoil, he is integrated.

He does not like fantasy, nor imagination,
He neglects all that is in the past, he does not escape
                                the present.
Calm and balanced, conscious moment by moment,
He moves in syntony with Existence, as it unfolds in time.

Ceaselessly, without stopping, permanently lucid and
                                attentive,
Like a burning flame he lights the present;
This is his true shelter, integrated into the "Whole".
Independent, he detaches from all that he has embraced.

Through a total Attention, he becomes a beacon of energy,
A universal force – pure and always renewing itself.
Right action is born out of wisdom,
Filled with Love, beyond the "ego" dimension.

When the phenomenon of Life – death – destiny incites one's curiosity, it means that the mysterious "something" hidden within the depth of one's being is suggesting the time to awaken to reality has arrived. Sooner or later, without any exception, each human being will come to this crucial point.

Our indifference or laziness, as we encounter this holy sign, will soon be sanctioned – so to speak – by various and increasingly painful events. Finally, as an effect of indolence, a great tragedy in our life – intellectually deemed as a misfortune – will finally propel us, against our will, on the path of spiritual evolution. On the outer layer of our surface consciousness a small incision has been made – a true window – attracting us into the mysterious depths of our being.

From now on, curiosity and interest stimulate our mind to find information, as well as to apply it, in order to fulfill the destiny of our incarnation. As knowing grows, so does the obligation to rigorously practice what we know.

Be aware, nevertheless, of the activity of surface consciousness or the "ego" – that is, the old man, rooted within us for millions of years as a selfish entity in conflict with himself and with the rest of the world! Seeing that its authority is endangered, the greedy and ambitious "self" uses a vast array of cunning and violent tricks, meant to set us off our course. Do not make any compromises with it! In its desperation, it will cry for mercy. Be firm, honest and determined in your decision to demolish its flimsy and hideous structure.

We set off on this path with simplicity, using all-encompassing Attention, which is, in fact, the Sacred within us in action. We just watch and listen to each reaction of the mind, triggered by Life's newness and mobility, on present moments in their eternal unfoldment.

The light of Attention dissipates the movements of the old; our being is united with Life itself, manifesting itself as Love and creative Intelligence. In this state, we have an infinite energy at our disposal, for we are "One" with the Boundless Infinite.

The divinity existent within each human being has never left us and it constantly invites us to use this simple path; any purpose, goals, ideals or pre-established faiths are completely excluded. Let us follow its holy invitation in all earnestness, by using the flame of Attention, from which all the benedictions ensue.

Happiness

Each human being on planet Earth is – consciously or unconsciously – searching for happiness with unlimited persistence and greed. Happiness appears as a mirage; we try countless ways in order to find it in the external world, with perseverance and determination; nevertheless, each time, the desired happiness finally results in a disappointing delusion.

Other, more subjective individuals turn to their inner world; in this case as well, their thirst for happiness is satisfied by sheer deceitful imagination. In each of our attempts to search for it, we start from what we know or imagine. Such happiness is always motivated by an object we anticipate or desire.

True happiness ensues indirectly. It always appears in a state of non-search. Practically, we do not know what happiness is, but, when the mind is completely silent, in a state of total passiveness, our whole being experiences harmony. In this state, as complete beings, integrated into Life, we are overwhelmed with an immense Joy and Happiness without cause.

Only when It appears as a real experience can we truly know Happiness and Its constant freshness, without turning It into a memory. Ever renewing itself, It is a natural gift offered to the individual who is free from his time-space structure. Only in this way do we discover the true Happiness that the wandering mind of the conditioned man has been searching for throughout the millennia.

All the topics in this volume, as well as in the previous books, constantly try to prove that the phenomenon of Happiness is a natural fact, accessible to each human being. The simplicity and innocence of the mind appear in a state of non-thinking; Happiness comes as a gift given to the being integrated into Life, detached from time and space.

***

Speaking about Truth, Reality, Love, God etc. by resorting to what others have said about it is the most profound error. Even if we mastered all the science and knowledge in the world intellectually, it would still be impossible for us to discover Reality, for the simple reason that knowledge is and will always remain limited, whereas Reality is boundless.

The ethical and moral degradation that we unfortunately encounter at every step in our present times originates in this defective manner of approaching that which is beyond our power of understanding.

Intellectual knowledge has its usefulness, but only on a physical plane; for instance, a technical mind can be employed in order to create economical progress or a certain technical application.

Spiritually, however, thinking, speaking or acting from our memory baggage can only strengthen the relative, small-minded and fearful authority of the fictitious "ego", further obscuring the Sacred. The negative consequences of the rule of the "self" are much too obvious to need mentioning.

It is only when the activity of the "ego" stops effortlessly and becomes silent, as it sees its own inability to encounter Truth, that the divine particle within us is revealed, manifesting itself as universal Love.

From that moment on, with a pure mind, in direct contact with reality unfolding in the present moment, we are in a permanent state of learning. With such a mind, we will never become old psychologically. We are, each time, a child-like innocence, learning perpetually.

***

The Absolute Truth is within you, waiting for you to allow it to manifest itself in all Its splendor. No one can offer It to you, and no one can open an external path of attaining It.

No book, philosopher, saint, master or theologian can give It to you. If anyone claims this, regard them with suspicion and do not let them exploit you. Neither prayers, nor offerings, nor bowing can persuade It to reveal Its presence within the limited structure of the worldly nature. There can be no auction in this regard.

The Absolute Truth requires constant, diligent work and earnestness from each practitioner, in order to realize the integration of being. By encountering everything that Life brings in our path with a lucid and innocent mind, without pursuing any purpose or models as hope or practical support, we spontaneously experience the silence or peace of the soul. In this "psychological emptiness", the true path towards the greatness of the Infinite opens.

In the new dimension – devoid of "I", "ego" or personality – we are the Absolute Truth, as choicelessness. In this state, we are also Love, Intelligence, Kindness, Beauty and Happiness. All these gifts form a single blissful bouquet – we live in perfect melting with the Sublime, the Eternal Boundlessness or God.

***

Let us remember that words, whether spoken or just silently creating the thinking process, regardless of their meaning, are and will always remain unsurpassable obstacles on the path of discovering our divine Nature. Only when the mind is humbly silent – seeing its power-lessness in the face of Infinity – then and only then does the Divinity within us reveal its presence as impersonal Love, directing us through intuitive impulses.

Beauty

A shining light, wondrous flashes,
A splendid calmness arising as a blessing.
When the being is whole – it melts into the Universe,
We encounter beauty, as a natural effect.

Inside and outside, we and beauty are one single
movement,
Ineffable purity, a perfect melting,
Just like the brightness of the Sun. When beauty is within us,
We also see beauty in flowers, in sand or even in mud,

In enchanting melodies, in moonlight or spring,
In a sunset or in a flying bird.
Thinking cannot create it, nor can it increase it,
It is not accumulated through time, strengthening the "ego".

In fact, it is simplicity, appearing spontaneously,
When the "ego" ceases momentarily;
The boundless man, detached from the past,
Encounters beauty beyond the known.

When beauty reigns in our depths, the whole being is
cheerful,
The face, the body radiates – everything glistens with
beauty;
When the moment is missed, we become physically and
psychologically agitated,
The knowing mind creates turmoil.

Therefore, be aware of your thoughts, the clouded mind,
Everything it knows or speaks is a pointless movement;
Perfectly conscious, all is transformed into harmony,
When ugliness is annulled by the Sublime and Joy.

The semantic meaning of beauty, as expressed in this poem, has no counterpart or term of comparison on the physical plane of existence. This beauty defines itself, through itself, as a mirroring, ensuing as the individual spirit melts into the Universal Mind. In this union, the spirit of the fortunate individual experiences moments of divine harmony and states of bliss which can only be partially communicated. No matter how expressive, words are and will remain nevertheless limited, unable to express the state of "being" one with the Whole.

We would not be able to encounter the beauty of a sunset or the beauty and perfume emanated by nature on a spring day, if we did not already have this beauty within us. When the beauty within us is revealed, we will also be able to see beauty in a flower, a leaf of grass or a grain of sand, or even in a clod of mud.

This beauty is not a result of thinking. Therefore, it cannot be imitated or cultivated in any form by the knowing mind. Neither imagination, nor effort, nor will can create it or express it in symbols.

Practically, it appears in simplicity when the knowing mind becomes humbly silent, as it has realized it cannot comprehend or encompass the immensity of life in its infinite diversity of manifestation.

In these blessed moments of high spirituality, the face lights up, the eyes sparkle, the whole being shines, in a state of joy. The physical body functions perfectly; through impulses, it heals any organic deficiencies.

The lack of beauty is easy to dispel, by any human being, if one is willing to point an attentive glance into the depth of one's being. The dysfunctional thinking process of the confused "ego" creates corresponding phenomena: a pointless waste of energy, stressful agitation with negative effects, both morally and physically. Therefore, point your total attention to the flow of thoughts which appear as reactions to the perpetual challenges of your daily life!

Correctly encountering these reactions leads to their demise. When all turmoil, agitation and ugliness disappears, a new climate reveals itself as peace and equilibrium of the soul. Beauty, as a state of pure harmony, brightness and joy without cause envelop our being, creating a new mentality.

This is the divine Real Man – existent in the deeper layers of consciousness within each of us – awaiting for us to discover him and to allow him to guide and lead us. Only in his presence do beneficial transformations occur. To this New Man we owe our encounter with true happiness.

The Thinker

Never reality, always a fiction,
A product of duality, through false action;
Thinking creates the thinker; its lack of consistency
Is born out of identification with thought.

Therefore thinking and the thinker have the same source,
They create the "self", striving for fulfillment;
The thinker can never transform the ever-changing thought
                                                    process,
It can only create a façade, a deceitful mask.

Centered on the "self", the thinker is purpose, fear, egoism,
It divides our being, incapable of any good;
When thinking stops, the thinker also disappears,
Peace ensues – an ever-renewing climate.

The old stops intervening, with its turbulent impulses,
For Attention dissolves it each moment.
As an integrated being, the individual lives in reality,
Always freshness, living as one, in utter simplicity.

Free from the past, fresh each moment,
Living in the present, he becomes a creative force,
He is Love, beauty, natural kindness,
A beacon for the entire world, a guide for integral life.

The thinker as an entity does not have a separate existence from thinking. The thinker and thinking are one and the same phenomenon. Let us try to decipher the mechanisms of thinking together, for this is where the thinker originates from.

For this purpose, let us take an example. In a competition, the name of the winner is announced; it is someone I know.

Therefore, I hear, interpret, assess and mentally record a fact. If I simply became aware of this fact, I would be happy for the winner's success. Unfortunately, this is not the case. A thought barges in, involuntarily; it separates me from that fact, and it spontaneously creates the envious entity and the feeling of envy: "Why him and not me?"

If a fact is filtered and mirrored by a thought, the thinker is also artificially created, as "ego" in action. It has no real support, for it is a fictitious entity. The appearance of the non-envious person – who scolds the envious person for the ugliness of his envy – is just another facet of the same entity.

All conflictual states originate here, in the conflict between "what is" – a real, undeniable fact – and "what we want it to be". This "something else" that we imagine or want, hoping it will give us certain benefits, is none other than the thinker, an effect of human egocentrism.

The thinker is similar to a king, sitting on its throne, at the center, constantly trying to create changes in the surrounding environment; its instrument is will, which, in its essence, is nothing but a desire wanting to be fulfilled. And desire is nothing but a thought, aspiring to take precedence over other thoughts.

Never, in any circumstances, can a thought create a radical transformation in the structure of the individual. A creation of time, always relative, it can only produce insignificant superficial changes. Thoughts are always at war with one another and cannot transcend themselves.

When man lives on the level of the "ego", aspiring to a spiritual ideal, he lays all his hopes of transformation on the thinking activity. From the very beginning, inside his being, a real psychological war ensues between what appears on the field of consciousness – as a reaction to the challenges of life – and what the aspirant wishes to become. On this battlefield, opposing thoughts fight each other fiercely in order to attain a final victory. The only result of this struggle is a more acute and deepened conflictual state and increased confusion.

If thoughts, deemed as perverse, become more and more rare, the practitioner concludes that he has reached spiritual heights or that he has gotten close to or even attained the model he was striving for. In fact, this is nothing but a camouflage, unconsciously accomplished by the Cerberus guarding the gates of consciousness: positive thinking; with each intervention, it buries the adverse thought even deeper into the subconscious.

One day, when this guardian is missing at his post or is tired of the constant strain, the repressed thought bursts out tempestuously, and no force can stop its effects. Constraint and repression did nothing but progressively strengthen its initial energies. The oppressed thought is like an enemy who retreats strategically, in order to accumulate enough force for an even more violent and destructive attack.

In conclusion, will and sustained effort can never create a real transformation and ennoblement of the human soul.

This noble task of emptying all the impurities which clutter the vessel of our consciousness belongs to the Sacred existent within us, manifesting itself as Love, goodness and beauty. It is never caught in the trap of thinking. It cannot be invoked, imagined or conquered with gifts. It appears naturally, undesired and uncaused, as soon as the mind ceases its activity. The void or psychological emptiness is the only modality of uniting our existence with the Absolute Truth.

Physical and Psychological Death

Through degradation and disease,
The body becomes tired, it disintegrates and dies.
It is a natural process – a natural effect,
All that is born, lives, grows and matures,
Finally it becomes weak and dies.

A completely different way of dying:
Psychological death is just as natural;
By completely forgetting our psychological baggage,
The "ego" – created in time – disappears.

The human being is free, integrated spontaneously.
Such a death is a path to true life,
All old patterns are dissolved,
As well as the hollow, arrogant thought process;
We understand the new, our spirit expands.

Death and life are happily united.
United as One, a perfect form.
There is no true life, if there is no death
To the past, to the old memory residues.
We die each moment, all is empty,

We embrace life as an eternal beginning.
The mind is sharp, clear and intelligent,
Living in the now, the mind is Wisdom,
A priceless climate of peace and security
Through spontaneous holy action.

In the common language characteristic of human under-standing, there are two distinct ways to die: physical death and psychological death.

Everything that appears in this world through birth, as a physical body, has a beginning, a period of development and growth, followed by a process of decline and degra-dation, because of old age or other unpredictable causes, finally leading to physical death.

In reality, the so-called death is nothing but the immortal aliveness detaching from the carnal body we were endowed with in the material dimension. In this evolutionary process, no matter how long it might take: years, days or mere seconds, everything is subject to a set of intrinsic unbending laws; all that exists in the universe obeys these laws.

From the perspective of the eternity of the aliveness, we are born to die and, when we die, we are reborn into another dimension, different from the one we have just left. For we come from eternity, from the source of immortality and, after a long journey in the world of matter, we shall return to the source we originated from.

Completely different from physical death, there is another kind of disappearance, more difficult to perceive: psychological death or the absolute silence of the thinking activity. Dying psychologically means consciously freeing ourselves from our memory residues, which chain us with emotional states, making it impossible to encounter and understand true life.

Only by being completely detached from that "which was" – in the present a mere image, a hollow shell – are we able to come into contact with "what is" in the now, enjoying the beauty and fragrance of the "aliveness" in its constant unfolding evolution.

Only by shattering all memories – the bricks which make up the walls of the "ego" – can we access the splendor of the Infinite.

This radical operation of eliminating the past can be accomplished by everyone, if we practice this simple understanding and encounter with life. What happened in the past is of no importance, nor is what we wish as a mental projection into the future.

Our whole being, perfectly lucid, points its total attention to each reaction arising from the sphere of thinking, as a consequence of challenges coming from either the inner world or the external world. In this simple encounter, silence or the "psychological void" ensues spontaneously, enabling us to correctly experience each event brought forth by the movement of life.

Any residues this experiment might leave behind are instantly eliminated as something old and outdated, preventing us from understanding the incoming moment. Thus, we die and resurrect perpetually, in direct connection with the flash of the moment.

Living in this state, we have a new, pure, innocent, limitless mind – detached from any limited patterns of thinking – completely identified with Wisdom. Through it, we are like a flame, burning continuously, fueled by the peace and security arising from the depth of our being.

Reaching this level of consciousness – through the death of the "ego" – the Sacred existent within each human being unites us with Eternity. From this new perspective, all individuals are the same; the Divine Spark leads our whole being, manifesting itself as uniqueness through Absolute Love.

The Flash of the Moment

Psychologically, we die each moment, as it appears and
vanishes,
Totally free from all that was or will be,
Practically, we are Infinite – in perfect harmony,
We are able to see, perceive directly what is false and
what is real.

Through this all-encompassing perception, taking place in
the present,
Without effort or will, each individual becomes a titan;
Living as One, he becomes universal.
This is the holy realization, integrated in the now.

In a flash, we detach from the lived moment,
Without returning to the past, without anticipating
the future,
We live only in the present, in direct contact with "what is",
Lucid, clear and open, a complete integration.

We leave the passing moment and we are reborn as
freshness,
A blissful being, true perfection.

Only by ourselves and through ourselves,
We find revelations, certainties, beyond any doubt,
When we connect and disconnect with each present moment,
Free from any imaginary future.

Understanding the phenomenon which consumes its
existence in the flash of the moment will illuminate and
reveal the mysterious meaning of life. For life, as we can
easily discover from experience, is like a flowing river, in
continuous movement. It never stops; any fixedness is
completely excluded by the very nature of the aliveness.

Life comes from eternity, moves in the present and flows
towards eternity. Thanks to this permanent mobility, life is
constant freshness and absolute newness from one moment

to another. For this reason, the moment is immensely important, as only in the space of the moment can we discover reality in its perpetual unfolding.

Our encounter with the moment is also an encounter with Eternity. In this short sparkle, we are integrated in the now; we practically disappear as a psychological entity created by time-space and we encounter Boundlessness. In other words, thinking understands its functional uselessness and it becomes completely silent; this silence unites us spontaneously with the Infinite.

When the old man – functioning anarchically – disappears, a new, favorable climate is created for the appearance of a new entity, manifesting itself as innocence and a state of pure consciousness. In fact, this is the real, true man, existent within each human being. Our duty is to give him the opportunity to reveal himself and his beneficial influence.

This pure reality, confirming our divine origin, has always been with us and it has never left us; it is eternally present through impulses of Love, beauty and kindness. We can discover it only through "Self-knowing", that is, through a direct, clear and disinterested encounter with our surface consciousness. By exposing this egoistic, chaotic and always conflictual entity with the light of Attention, it becomes silent, and the moment provides this wonderful realization.

A correct encounter with the moment consists of attachment followed by detachment, free from any memory baggage. Therefore, the phenomenon of knowing ensues spontaneously, free from any cerebral recordings, and is also finalized without accumulating any information. Everything is dissipated so that, each time, we are in a perfect state of innocence and freshness, similar to life in its perpetual movement.

Levels of Consciousness

The human being's existence expands on seven planes,
With precise laws of experience and comprehension.
Thought and emotion are a clear sign
Of our level of consciousness, on this wonder-filled path.

As our frequency becomes less limited
Emotional experience opens towards sacred levels of
consciousness.
Spiritual evolution is the path to perfection –
Just as we were in the beginning: One with God.

The first plane is the physical, gained by birth,
God manifested through matter.
Each plane is experienced and comprehended
When the individual awakens in the moment.

In the State of Simply Witnessing, we live the whole range,
The experiencer and Life melt into One.
Each being is capable of total understanding –
Our birthright from God – as well as total freedom.

"Self-knowing" is a treasure, absolutely necessary
On this plane of illusions and carnal instincts.
Dissipating ignorance requires a lot of discipline,
Encounter it constantly, with a lucid Attention.

The second plane, the astral, is twinned with emotional pain,
Remorse, blame – we condemn ourselves, through
                                        ourselves,
Seeing our errors from our last incarnation,
We experience hell, through our own programming.

The third plane, the plane of *power* – its characteristic: the
                                        search for domination:
Blind faiths and theories rule our life,
Certainty is used as the unique point of view,
Its victims are deceived by ephemeral illusions.

The fourth plane, the plane of *Incomplete Love,*
We experience different aspects of Light
Occurring in the depth of our being,
But it is not manifest through our instinctual impulses.

The fifth plane is a celestial paradise,
Here, all is Light and all our desires are instantly fulfilled.
A special climate
Where each person experiences real happiness.

As each desire is effortlessly granted
We linger on this plane for very long periods of time.
Dreaming is comfortable, it overwhelms us,
Thus beings forget about experiencing higher planes.

The sixth plane is a level of Consciousness united with Life,
We melt into the great Whole;
This experience takes us into Infinity
An open door absorbs us into the Limitless.

By becoming one with the Whole – our beloved Father
Represents the next plane, the seventh.
On this final plane, The Sky – as Christ called it –
We and the Father are One, a harmonious Unity.

In the seventh Sky – an Infinite and All-encompassing Light
Within us, a Spark of Light, existent through Itself,
Soul and Spirit as one – a State of Pure Consciousness.
Pure Reason, Pure Life and Pure God, in all Its being.

Living persistently, moment to moment,
United with the Whole of Existence, permanently and
                                        inherently,
We will certainly experience the State of Enlightenment,
The Realization of Wisdom, Love in eternal movement.

All human beings are destined to reach this supreme goal
As incarnated Gods, free from all limitations.
Kindness, Beauty, Happiness and Love
Are always available to us, as a spontaneous experience.

When we find out about these things, it is not a mere
                                                    coincidence,
But a certain sign that we have reached a certain spiritual
                                                    maturity
To apply and practice what we read in this verse,
For this knowledge compels us to experience purity.

Never postpone, never say "I cannot"!
The responsibility is solely yours, as well as the regret
When you leave this body during your fictitious death!
In fact, only the body dies when the Spirit deserts it, with
                                                    all its vitality.

Finally we must remember a certain, essential fact:
As long as we live on this earth, incarnated in a body,
We have the ability to experience directly
All seven planes of consciousness – through an integral
                                                    comprehension.

Our burning desire, persistence, work and diligence
Will transmute our state, opening us to other planes of
                                                    existence,
Creating a new Man, with universal powers,
Pioneer of a new world, ruled by purely moral and holy
                                                    impulses.

There is another level of existence, difficult to imagine,
Where naive entities linger erroneously;
Some think they have died when the body died,
Although their thought confirms they continue to exist
psychologically.

Others, the fanatical faithful, believe what they
have been told,
That they only have one life; in deep lethargy they wait
to be awakened
By the second coming of the Messiah, creating a kingdom
Lasting a thousand years. This is clear stupidity!

Both the former and the latter live in darkness
And refuse any support of help and Wisdom;
They exist on the first and second plane – as social
conscience,
Trapped in time, in a dual existence.

The human being's existence spans seven planes of existence or seven skies; each level has its characteristic experiences and perceptions. Thought and feeling – as well as our State of Being – are an indication of our level of Consciousness on the wondrous path of spiritual evolution.

As our thinking becomes more limitless, we experience higher levels of existence. Evolution is a sign, an indication of our current stage of being on the journey of returning Home and becoming One with the Creative Divine.

The first plane is the physical; here, we live in association with dense matter, as God in raw material form. On this plane – as incarnated beings – we have access to all the other planes and we are able to experience and comprehend them when we encounter the movement of Life as simple witnesses. In this state, we and Life melt together and function as One Whole. Every human being has been endowed by the Creative Divine with all-encompassing understanding, as well as Absolute Freedom.

"Self-knowing" is the birthright of all human beings and it is absolutely necessary on this plane of illusions led by carnal instincts. This attainment requires a lot of self-discipline, in order to expose the ignorance and confusion created by this fleeting and illusory world. On this plane, we will permanently use all-encompassing, lucid and disinterested Attention, encountering all that Life brings in our path, pleasant or unpleasant events.

The second plane is the astral; here, suffering, remorse and self-blame are stored, connected to our deeds and behavior during the previous incarnation. Therefore, we ourselves create our own hell, through our own programming – by condemning ourselves for our past mistakes and so-called sins.

The third: the plane of power; its characteristic is domination. All the mystics who rely on the content of their faith dwell on this plane. They try to impose their beliefs through verbal persuasion.

The fourth plane: the plane of incomplete Love. On this plane we find all the human beings who have experienced the depths of Love and have been unable to externalize it, because of the powerlessness of their nature.

The fifth plane is a paradise in the sky. This plane is like a magical realm, filled with divine music, suspended gardens etc. Here, all desires are spontaneously fulfilled, providing everyone with a state of contentment and happiness. As each wish is immediately granted, we can dwell on this plane for a long period of time. The temptation of such an existence is so mesmerizing that some Souls live on this plane for thousands of years, completely forgetting that there are any superior levels of existence.

The sixth plane is a level of Consciousness in perfect Union with the Existential Whole. In fact, our purpose or psychological goal on this plane is to encounter the Infinite. Here lies the gate to Absolute Truth, absorbing us and uniting us with the Whole, anticipating the next plane.

The seventh plane can be described as An Infinite and All-pervading Light. Within us, a pure Spark appears, existent through Itself. Here we are Spirit-Soul – a State of Pure Consciousness. We are also Pure Reason, Pure Life and Pure God within our whole being.

A natural question each individual needs to ask is: How can we reach the State of Enlightenment, a true characteristic of Wisdom and unconditional Love in eternal movement?

It is every human being's destiny – since our creation – to attain this wonderful realization as incarnated Gods, living as Kindness, Beauty, Joy and Happiness. The very fact that we have come to know about the existence of such a state is an undeniable sign that we have reached a sufficient level of maturity to apply and practice this wonderful perspective of living in utter purity.

Therefore, let us not postpone this accomplishment and not accept our inability to attain this wondrous realization. When we leave this plane – during the fictitious death, a mere detachment from the physical body – we will utterly regret not fulfilling the invitation to self-perfection.

Finally, let us remember an essential fact: on this plane of existence (as incarnated beings) we have the capacity to truly experience all seven levels of Existence. Our personal work, diligence, persistence and burning desire will create a beneficial and exceptional transformation. A new Man will appear, with universal powers, endowed with highly

moral and spiritual qualities. As each individual is transformed, a new world will be created, superior to the world
we live in during our present times.

Before ending, let us mention another level of the
invisible world, a difficult and imaginary climate, where
naive entities dwell in a dark environment created by their
erroneous beliefs. These souls believe they have died
during the death of the physical body, even though their
thinking says otherwise. We are talking about the fanatic
religious believers who, during their incarnation, had the
conviction that they have only one life on Earth and that,
after they die, they need to wait to be resurrected by the
savior Jesus Christ, who will create a kingdom lasting a
thousand years.

This whole fictional story is nothing but an ineptitude
invented by religion.

Well-wishing spirits who have tried to help them did
not manage to dispel their profound fanaticism; therefore,
they shall continue to remain in darkness and isolation,
which they have created themselves, through imagination.

Abandon Yourself to Life

Life is Sacredness, the Divine, God or Infinity;
Any names are meaningless,
As long as there is no real experience, no true meeting
And melting with Life, any description is hollow.

Incarnated on planet Earth, our duty is to realize this
                                                    encounter,
Each living moment, to become integrated into Life.
How can we encompass and comprehend limitless Reality?
How can there be real understanding through old
                                                    knowledge?

No matter how cultured, the mind is a limited pattern,
Utterly unable to embrace the Infinite!
What can we do? Is there a path to fulfillment?
Not at all! For any path is based on the thinking process!

Will, effort or faith are of no use
When encountering the Sacredness of Life;
All three are a manifestation of the small-minded "ego",
With each activity – it enforces its prison.

When you discover the truth of human powerlessness,
The mind is enlightened – spontaneously – you stop.
The mind – the whole "ego" – is silent, the Sacred within
                                                    us is revealed,
In this revelation, Love envelops and overwhelms us.

From now on, we are guided by this Reality,
Everything it encounters, it resolves, in simplicity;
A new man with a new mind is born,
Through him, the whole world gradually evolves.

Abandoning ourselves to Life, we become Its instrument,
In direct contact with the moment, we become whole;
Our being becomes one, we are pure wisdom,
In everything we think, speak or do.

Life is Sacredness, Absolute Truth or God. We can call it by any name. Words have no other purpose than to facilitate communication between human beings. Whatever symbol we might use, it will never encompass Reality; the mere symbol is hollow, devoid of content.

The true purpose of our incarnation in a body is to accomplish this perfect encounter, union and integration with Life. We are in constant communion with It, moving moment to moment.

Can the ordinary man – with his mind made of memory residues – encounter or comprehend the Reality of Life?

Of course not! The human mind – no matter how cultured – is and will always remain a limited structure. What can we do in this circumstance? Is there a certain path we can follow?

Not at all! Any path towards liberation is also based on thinking or on deceitful faiths. Neither will, nor effort, nor repeating formulas, nor sublimation are of any use in the encounter with the Sacredness of Life.

The moment we become aware of all this, through self-inquiry, we realize the powerlessness of our mind and, instantaneously, we stop. This is the crucial moment; when the mind and the whole movement of the "ego" become silent, the Sacred existent within us reveals Itself by Itself. In the simplicity of this encounter, Love overwhelms our whole being.

From now on, we allow this Holy Reality to guide us; everything It encounters is dissipated by Its mere presence.

A new man, with a new mind, embraces day-to-day life; both we and the whole world evolve, morally and spiritually.

By abandoning ourselves to Life, we become a mere instrument – in direct contact with the unfolding moment, we are integrated, as a complete, united "Whole". Thought, speech and deed are always based on absolute, intelligent and hallowing intuitive impulses.

Happiness Is Independent of Age

When we encounter Happiness, we live in timelessness,
The "ego" has disappeared, with its dual illusion.
Who is left to evaluate this state?!
For the Sacred within us and the world are One.

Do we see this from experience, or only intellectually?
We need to give the answer ourselves, inquire into its
                                                reality.
From birth until death, everyone searches for Happiness,
We do not encounter it anywhere, as long as we rely on
                                                thinking.

Happiness has no motivations and it is unlimited,
By its nature, It is infinite, free from imagination.
It is revealed by itself through itself, in Its immensity,
Our duty, in utter simplicity, is to create a space for it.

When the mind is completely silent – illuminated by
                                                    Attention,
Silence creates true integration;
From now on, the being is Infinite and Sacredness,
Absorbed into the Universe, a Supreme Union.

In this state – as "Absolute Purity"
Happiness is inherent, it comes as a gift.
A moment of Happiness is priceless,
For such a person, youth or old age has no relevance.

The moment we encounter true Happiness, we are in fact outside time and space. The "ego" – with its intrinsic duality – has completely disappeared.

If the "ego" does not exist anymore, who can evaluate this happy fulfillment?

In that moment, the Sacred within us, also existent in the whole universe, becomes one "Whole" and a Unique movement, in a permanent renewal.

Do we truly experience this union, or do we merely understand it intellectually? You alone can answer this question.

Each human being – from the moment of birth until the moment of the so-called death – persistently searches for this mysterious Happiness. Unfortunately, most people make the mistake of searching for it with the thinking mind.

Because Happiness has no motivations, It is not part of the limited world. Its nature is infinite; therefore the knowing mind cannot encounter It, or understand It, or imagine It.

If the mind – contaminated by arrogance – nevertheless

tries to accomplish this encounter, the result can be nothing but an insolent fantasy.

Happiness comes to us by Itself, and It envelops our whole being when the mind becomes humble and silent, as it has understood its inability to encounter the Unknown. Lucid Attention – with Its flashes – dissipates all the darkness, as well as the baggage of the dysfunctional mind.

In the empty space of peace or no-mind, our being is extended into Infinity; in that moment, the Divinity within us reveals we are one with the Source of the Sacred. In conclusion, let us add that in the environment of "Pure Consciousness", Happiness is present as a natural fulfillment and It is unlike anything that can be found in this perishable world.

The individual who experiences the phenomenon of Happiness is not influenced, in any way, by the number of his years – whether few or many – connected to this ephemeral life in association with the world of matter.

In the "Psychological Emptiness" We Encounter Reality

"Psychological emptiness" and Reality,
Two words – one experience – originating in Purity;
The realized individual – an integrated being
In direct contact with the Sacredness of Life – a total
melting.

The "psychological void" is peace, perfect stillness,
The mind is humble, silent, free from guilt,
For it has understood its inability to know limitless
                                                    Eternity.

Can the mind annul itself, through itself?
Can it dissolve itself and create "Emptiness"?
Never, in any circumstances, for it is a state of constant
                                                    turmoil,
Agitation is its nature, conditioned by time.

The Stillness of the mind ensues when the mind is
                                                    illuminated,
When all-encompassing Attention dissipates its
                                                    movement;
In its light – the mind perishes, for it is not real,
It is but a shadow, hollow and deceitful.

"Emptiness" – a mere window opening towards Infinity;
The individual is absorbed into it,
He lives the Absolute Truth, spontaneously,
It cleanses and transforms all past knowledge.

Here we discover Reality – a Divine Realm –
Accessible to anyone, through a direct experience.
The whole purpose of our incarnation lies in this
                                                    encounter,
In stillness, the individual becomes Love.

Through this simple presence, we experience Truth,
It transforms the individual and the whole of existence,
Creating a new world of kindness and honesty,
An earthly Paradise – Life is perpetual newness.

Psychic Pollution

The growing collective misery of our present day,
The general movement of arrogance, the collective
madness,
Insatiable greed, never-ending search for fulfillment,
Senseless violence, creating countless wars,

All originates within us, just as force originates in the atom,
The lack of reason has its source in the individual,
Through thought, speech and deed, we influence the whole
world;
We are all one, in constant communication.

Psychically, we are united with the world, just like the
water in the ocean,
There is no separation; moment after moment, year after
year,
Through our egocentrism, we pollute the whole world,
We are partly responsible for the evil we have created.

When we encounter ourselves with the flame of Attention,
Watching all thoughts, impulses from the past – intruding
                                    in the present,
All that was is dissipated, with all its evilness,
As well as the ugly "ego" – a real calamity.

Free from the past, the individual lives in the "now",
Integrated into life, he creates a different world.
The person who experiences truth is like a lightning rod,
A true creator in the present;

He dissolves the pollution and creates a new energy,
Without thoughts and without effort, he vanquishes
                                    psychic refuse,
The whole world is transformed when the "ego" is
                                    dissipated,
Without any need for reform, from an imaginary past.

Melting into life, without yesterday or tomorrow,
Beyond time and space, holy action is born,
Without asking questions, without resorting to thinking,
The experiencer of truth becomes a beacon of Love.

Industrial development, particularly the chemical industry,
has caused an accelerated degradation of the environment
we live in. Our health is more or less affected by the air we
breathe, by the water we drink and the food we ingest, as
well as by noise pollution.

Based on undeniable arguments, scientists have demon-
strated the danger threatening each and every one of us.

Through a series of persistent interventions, they have persuaded political leaders to take certain measures, in order to maintain the degradation of the environment at low levels.

Independently from these protective measures, humans as well as all other living beings are endowed with inbuilt physiological mechanisms, enabling them to adapt to the new conditions of polluted nature. Species and individuals adjust to the new circumstances, according to their adaptation abilities, which differ from individual to individual, depending on the genetic makeup.

On a physical level, this phenomenon is well known and very obvious. Let us see what the situation is on a psychological level. Is psychic pollution a well-known fact? Do we realize that, through the activity of our chaotic thinking, we co-create all the conflictual states existent in the world, such as violence, crimes and wars?

It might seem incredible, but a mere quarrel or an irritating discussion with our wife, daughter, neighbor or workmate has a negative influence on a planetary level. Our state of irritation attracts similar energies and adds to the already existent immense flow of hate and violence, amplifying its intensity.

Therefore, unknowingly and unwillingly, we indirectly participate in all the murders, wars and any act of violence taking place on planet Earth. It is a natural consequence because, psychologically, we and the entire world are one unity. We are – to use a simile – like the drops of water in an ocean, forming one single homogenous mass.

Because of this unity, the energy we emit as thought waves will finally return upon us. Between us and the rest of the world, there is a permanent ebb and flow, an interchange by which we are influenced and we influence.

If so far things are clear – understood not just intellectually, by simply accepting information and data provided by someone else, but comprehended from personal experience – a question follows: What can we do about it? How can we free ourselves from this vicious circle?

The thinking activity, as well as imagination and efforts of will, projected egocentrically, are of no use to us. On the contrary, thinking itself is a polluting factor and can do nothing but amplify this phenomenon. This simple discovery, attained individually, is a good start. Therefore, we discover by ourselves that the "ego" fiction or the surface consciousness – conditioned by the dimension of time – is responsible for all the chaos existent today in the world.

If we see facts and phenomena as they are, without any other intervention, they are spontaneously dissipated. In the emptiness of the thinking activity or the psychological void, we discover that we nevertheless continue to exist as pure consciousness. In this new state, we live outside time, without dimensions; with an all-encompassing, clear and lucid Attention, we move in perfect harmony, renewing itself from one moment to another.

The true man existent in the depth of our being reveals himself, fueled by his self-sufficient energy. He is beauty, kindness, Love and absolute Truth. This is the reality of the blissful man and it represents a true benediction for the whole of humanity. His beneficial influence on the world is considerable. In his presence, all the relative energies creating psychic pollution are – purely and simply – dissipated.

Let us emphasize that it is only when we function on this level that we are truly complete whole beings – body and mind – in perfect unity. In such moments, the body functions naturally, creating a state of good health.

Immensity

Eyes cannot perceive it,
Mind cannot imagine it,
Thought cannot grasp it
Through absurd opinions.

It is impossible
To give it any form or shape.
We cannot discover it,
With the knowing mind.

No matter how cultured,
The mind is limited,
For it was created by time,
It will always remain confined.

Two completely distinct worlds,
Different in their essence;
It is impossible to compare them
Through deceptive thinking.

On the one hand, the limited,
Where thinking is the master;
On the other, the Infinite,
Where all knowledge vanishes.

When we live in limitedness,
Life is intertwined with fear;
Conformism and contradictions
Born out of mind patterns.

When we melt into the Boundless,
We transcend the "self".
We are peace, harmony,
Happiness and joy.

There are no problems, no conflicts,
All illusion is shattered,
For, in utter silence,
There is Love and light.

From now on, we are Immensity,
We move in a timeless state;
A sacred blessing,
An invitation to become integrated.

The everyday life of the ordinary man unfolds within the
boundaries which limit and define his field of perception.
Intellectual or material possessions create his personality –
egocentric by its very nature – and prevent him from

encountering anything other than a boring, commonplace and confused existence.

Psychologically, he is the product of the social environment; he reacts mechanically, according to the moral and ethical conditioning impressed by educational factors. Chained in this manner, he is often in conflict with himself as well as with his surrounding environment; stress and turmoil create his life, a formless, meaningless subsistence.

Trapped in this pattern of living, in which intellect creates his essential character, the human being is unable to come into contact with and comprehend Immensity. We cannot perceive it with our eyes, or through imagination, no matter how hard the most fantastic mind might attempt to do so.

The thinking activity, with its various concepts, ideas, opinions, cannot perceive or grasp Reality, in any circumstance or form. This incapacity of the human mind is nothing but a consequence of its limited structure, unable to encompass Boundlessness.

The two states completely exclude each other. The presence of one makes the presence of the other impossible.

As long as the human being functions as an "ego", conditioned by time and space, which create its structure, he is and will always remain a prisoner of the limited.

Discovering this truth, through a lucid-attentive all-encompassing perspective, without any intervention, naturally leads to the spontaneous silence of the "ego". Peace, silence and harmony envelop our whole being – body and mind – and we transcend into the second state – we are integrated into Immensity.

It is only on this level of existence that we can understand, through a direct experience, the meaning of the expressions: going beyond the human condition, integration into universality, love, beauty, intelligence, the state of enlightenment, unconditional happiness, the purity of the mind, union with God etc.

In conclusion, psychological emptiness ensues naturally when we understand, directly and intuitively, our limited way of functioning; thus, we melt into Immensity and experience the Sacred.

The Surprise of Liberation

The liberation from the "self", from the human condition,
Is always a surprise, a spontaneous event;
The knowing mind blocks it
Through the personal energies of the chained "ego".

What does the individual do with his knowing mind?
He chains and enslaves his eternal being;
This is what humanity has been doing since ancient times,
We can see the results in the possessed minds.

Knowledge without practice – as "direct Knowing",
A correct experience of "just being" –
Only strengthens the possession, degrading our being,
Through vanity, pride and arrogance.

Here, I am trying to describe this phenomenon,
As I encountered and experienced it.
One morning, the very moment I was waking up,
I was surprised to notice that my thinking had changed.

The mind and everything I encountered were a complete
unity,
I was moving as a Whole – a perfect understanding;
The hazy mind, running towards yesterday or tomorrow
Had become silent, acting as one!

The whole phenomenon is a mystery, unknown by the
mind,
In the beginning, for some time, I could not name it,
Although I had read about it in books, described in detail;
Through flashes of intuition, came the comprehension.

Here is what followed, without any acts of will on my part,
All I had used previously: methods, practices, faiths,
Naturally detached from me and disappeared,
I started functioning differently, as a complete, integrated
man.

The previous mind, narrow in its imagination,
Had suddenly become Infinite – Universal;
From the depth of my being, a definite impulse came,
To write about this state using verse, in total harmony.

"Self-knowing" is a message to humanity,
As the spiritual evolution of our divine being,
By constantly encountering the behavior of the mind,
Conditioned by time.

To enable a clearer understanding, prose is also used,
Each title is explained, intertwined with experience.
A state of Pure Consciousness, an absolute union,
Body, mind and the Sublime – a perfect Oneness!

All-encompassing Attention and its spontaneity
Is the universal key, opening the path to Eternity,
Shattering and dissolving the "ego" and its fortress,
Holding us prisoners from times immemorial.

The Liberation from the "self", from our human conditioning recorded throughout countless past lives,
dominating us and turning us into robots – is always a
surprise phenomenon, occurring spontaneously.

Do we realize that we live and act as prisoners of our
recorded past, preserved in the library of our mind? If we
are unaware of this fact, this title will appear irrelevant,
absurd even.

As long as we consider ourselves to be just a physical
body, directed by a personal mind, the word "Liberation"
appears meaningless. Liberation from what or whom?

But if we realize, from our own experience and
perception, that the mind and the body become old, they
deteriorate, are dissipated and perish, this very discovery
compels us to inquire deeper into its reality. Here is what
we discover: "our true Nature" is neither the body, nor the

mind. We can only encounter It in a state of Pure Consciousness or "being".

Therefore, our memory accumulations create the "personal self"; it acts and functions within its confined shell which protects and limits its understanding; it always follows an agenda related to "me" and "mine". Limited and possessive, the "ego" prevents us from discovering "our true Nature" – immortal, without beginning and without end.

The knowing mind, wrongly deemed as the absolute value, has been leading humanity since very ancient times; it has been preserved in the form of tradition and transferred from generation to generation, until our present times. But mere knowledge, without directly applying and experiencing the truth, can only strengthen the egoic possession and degrade us morally.

The knower is a creation of knowledge; he overvalues himself and sees everything through the lens of the "ego", regarding his fellow beings with disdain and arrogance. The whole psychological climate, so obvious in the world of today – in the individual's relationship with himself as well as with the environment – demonstrates, in an undeniable, obvious way, our erroneous psycho-somatic approach to the eternal flow of Life.

In what follows, I will try to describe the phenomenon of Liberation as it revealed itself to me; I was only a subject on which this particular operation was performed. One morning, waking up from my sleep, I noticed that, intellectually, I was functioning differently from the night before. My wandering mind, always oscillating between the past and the future, had stopped its wandering. From then on, body, mind and soul formed a perfect unity; I was functioning as a Whole, perfectly conscious of what I was doing in the moment.

The surprise caused by this phenomenon was so great that, in the beginning, I was unable to name it, although I had read enough literature about Enlightenment, Liberation or the shattering of the "ego". This name came from intuition, spontaneously, as a flash, in a moment of profound silence.

Here is what followed, without any desire or will on my part. Everything happened through an inner illumination; its effects dissipated all the practices I had done previously, such as methods, faiths, efforts of will, repeating formulas etc. All these simply detached from my mind and left an emptiness of knowing, as my whole being was functioning as "One", present in the now.

My previous, limited mind, based on knowledge, had been replaced with an Infinite, Universal Mind. The same day, I received an intuitive impulse, or an order, to write about all this, expressing it in verse, always in direct connection with the experience of this phenomenon.

This message is offered to the whole of humanity; I consider myself to be a simple instrument, my role: to simply describe it. The purpose of this message is the spiritual recovery of humanity, by discovering the divinity within each individual. Practicing this message does not require any effort. All we need to do is to simply become conscious of the chaotic movement of the mind and its conditioning.

An attentive encounter with the movement of the mind, such as: thoughts, images, desires, feelings, makes them disappear instantly. As you can see, liberation from the past is realized from the very first moment. The flash of the moment is a true blow to the fortress of the "ego" whose prisoners we are, possessed by our memory possessions.

"Self-knowing" is not a method, nor a philosophical concept, nor a religious belief, because all these start from a purely egoistic center of interest, pursuing an ideal or goal to accomplish, using desire or effort directed by will or faith as a mental projection.

In order to facilitate the understanding of the message – as an interior impulse, received from the dimension of the Infinite – I was asked to use prose as well, also in connection with the direct experience of the state I had described in verse.

The only instrument we use in this encounter with ourselves is all-encompassing, lucid, disinterested and spontaneous Attention. It is the Sacred itself within us; in a flash, it dissipates, cleans and disintegrates the energies of the "ego" and its whole structure, holding the ignorant man prisoner since the very ancient times of his historical past.

The Evolution of Consciousness

The path towards discovering the Absolute Truth is written in the destiny of every form of existence within the whole Universe. The psycho-somatic evolution scale includes all its components, from the most primitive forms of existence to the most elevated beings.

Man has been evolving for millions of years, experiencing all three forms of manifestation of the objective world. In the beginning he was a rock, then a plant, an animal and finally, at the peak of evolution on this planet, he is incarnated as a human being. All these forms of existence have their source in the same Cosmic Energy, also called Truth or God. In order to further facilitate understanding, we can also call it Life, or the existent Aliveness, which can be more or less perceived in the three life forms we have mentioned earlier.

As far as gross matter is concerned – for instant, a rock – it is only apparently motionless, inert and dead; its actual reality is completely different. Scientists have proved that within each grain of sand there is ceaseless movement. This movement, in its intrinsic energy, is manifested as perfect coherence, maintaining the integrity of its structure.

Therefore, we find this perpetual movement – the Aliveness in action – in the rock as well; it is also endowed with intrinsic sensitivity. Hitting or performing an act of violence against the rock causes it to suffer and lament the pain induced by the external factor. Similarly, excessive cold or heat has a negative impression on the rock, just as it has a negative influence on any living being. Naturally, at our current level of vibration, we are unable to perceive its response.

Therefore Life, or the Aliveness existent in all and everything that exists, is equally present in a rock as it is in a human being. This Universal Energy and Absolute Perfection, the source of everything, is the driving force behind all that exists.

The only thing that differentiates us human beings from all other existential forms is appearance – the external form, manifesting itself in its infinite diversity.

That "Atom of divine existence" which can be found in each individual – unites us not only with our fellow human beings, but also with all the other forms of objective manifestation found in the Universe. The "spiritual Particle" in the rock will also one day be incarnated in a human body, through the slow and long process of evolution.

Passing from one form of existence to another, from an inferior species to a superior one, can only take place through suffering and death. We die in one form and resurrect in another superior form of manifestation.

Nowhere, in the boundless Universe, are there static forms. Everything is in perpetual movement and constant evolution. The divine creation has never stopped. Imperfection follows a continuous impulse towards perfection, generated by the "Divine Spark" found in all existential forms of manifestation, both visible and invisible.

***

In the immensity of the Universe there is only one Energy; human beings, in the course of their existence as incarnated beings, have used different names to describe It: Cosmic Energy, Jehovah, God, Allah, Absolute Truth etc.

This unique Energy was not created by anyone. Therefore, It has always existed. It has no beginning and It will have no end. It comes from Eternity and It flows constantly and perpetually towards the same Eternity, as an independent Force with an infinite potential of movement and creation.

Present everywhere and in all that exists, seen or unseen by our senses, this energy also exists within each human being. Therefore, no man can affirm or claim that he has more Divinity than his fellow human beings.

In no circumstance can we perceive it with our senses. It cannot be understood, conceptualized or trapped in formulas using the intellect or the knowing mind. All these – through their limited nature – cannot encompass and comprehend "That which is limitless" or Infinity.

As we mentioned earlier, when our mind realizes its own powerlessness, it becomes humble and silent; through this attitude, it gives the Divinity within us the opportunity to manifest Itself in all Its intrinsic splendor. Therefore, Divinity can only be discovered by the Divinity existent within us.

In this state of happiness we discover – through direct, personal experience – that we were never separated from this Eternal Oneness. By encountering It in a real way, we become creative beings, able to radically transform our powerless nature, with beneficial influences on the external world as well.

Therefore, the world we live in – overwhelmed with contradictions and conflictual states – is the result of each person's dysfunctional behavior; it can only be healed by starting a transformation with ourselves.

Let us not deceive ourselves, by blaming someone else

for the degradation we see within us and around us. For only we – through everything we think, speak or do – create the psychological climate within us, around us and generally, on the entire surface of the planet, with influences on the entire Universe.

The real meaning of life as incarnated beings lies in discovering our Divine Nature, manifesting itself as impersonal Love. It is only in this fortunate circumstance that the vessel of (surface and profound) consciousness empties all the residues it has accumulated during our profound ignorance as egocentric beings, severely dominated by the illusion of ephemeral things.

As the long series of incarnations ends, the "Divine Spark", which has always been with us and has never left us, returns to the Source of Sources, from where – millions of years ago – it descended in order to experience the world of matter.

Listening

Have you ever considered listening
And the possibility of listening to yourself?
When compulsive thinking is not aware of its
                                  mechanicalness,
It becomes manifest through speech.

Spoken words coming from the knowing mind,
Thousands of facts and bits of information,
An unstoppable flow which overshadows the present.
We are disconnected from "what is", in the now.

By directing your attention towards your interior,
An immense ear that is content to just listen,
Spontaneously, we attain clear listening,
Instrument of peace and transformation.

When, in utter silence, we listen to our depths,
The "ego" disappears, we are one with "emptiness".
Inner and outer become one,
All is united in spontaneous peace.

Only through listening do we become free of the past,
Which keeps us prisoners, chained by pleasure,
Constantly escaping fear and what we deem unpleasant;
Thus, the spell we are under is shattered.

Simple listening dissipates all,
The human being attains priceless freedom,
Without "ego", we become pure Love
Expanding into Immensity – a Sacred fulfillment.

Listening and watching melt together as one, creating a single movement. The actual practice of listening is not easy. We have great difficulty listening to a man speaking, the noise of the street, the chirping of a bird or a song.

The contact with the impressions coming from the external world, in the form of wavelengths, involuntarily and almost instantaneously sets the engine of the thinking process – a creation of the past – into motion. The thinker starts to analyze, assess, judge and draw conclusions.

Ordinarily, we are unable to listen to one another because of our so-called values, extracted from the conclusions of the content of our memory recordings, viewed through the lens of pleasure or pain.

When husband and wife live together for long periods of time, for instance, listening to and understanding one another becomes difficult. Because of habit, created throughout time, we have already created images of each other which come into play as soon as we are in contact. In fact, only our images meet and not the true, real man, as a whole, complete perception.

For a specialized person, a musicologist for instance, it is very difficult, almost impossible to listen to a concert he knows by heart, as well as the technique of expression. The vast range of knowledge he has in that particular field becomes a serious impediment preventing true listening, in this case or in general. The musicologist will listen more to himself than to the concert. He will constantly interpret what he hears through the lens of his knowledge in the field. Furthermore, mentally, he will also anticipate excerpts from that particular music score. This happens, of course, because he already knows what follows, as well as how the music should be played.

In order to accomplish true listening, we need to completely dissolve all the reactions that appear in the field of consciousness each time we come into contact with life in all its complex aspects, as perpetual freshness and surprise from one moment to another.

Reactions are dissolved through a simple, direct contact, without making any comments or efforts of will in order to make them disappear.

It is only when equilibrium and harmony ensue in absolute silence, unwanted and unforced, that we will truly be able to listen not only with our ears, but with our whole being. Through the act of listening, we are in a direct connection with all the manifestations of sound, both in the external world as well as within us, as thoughts and images. In fact, a perfect melting is attained between us and the person who speaks, the song or the external noise.

In this fortunate circumstance, the "ego" and its whole memory baggage is completely dissolved. From now on, as an integral being, we manifest ourselves fully as creative Love, transforming and ennobling the conditioned egocentric structure, trapped in time, living in a perpetual state of conflict and fear.

The Fulfillment

"Empty" of time and space,
We are "Sacred Unity",
Body and mind as one,
Integrated into Eternity.

Our purpose on Earth
Lies in this realization,
As an intrinsic law
Based on Love.

There are no expectations,
No desires, images,
Just a direct, immediate experience
Writing Life's Holy pages.

Clear-attentive, we just watch "what is",
The mind frequently strays,
Running like mad,
Inebriated by time.

This encounter dissipates it,
Integration ensues.
A supreme experience
Through it – we become Eternity.

Here, in few words, we can experience the wholeness of being. Empty of memory residues – created by time and space – we are Sacred Simplicity. Body, mind and spirit together form a unique "Whole", and we naturally melt into Eternity.

The true purpose of our existence as incarnated beings consists of this simple realization; Love reveals itself as the essence of our true nature. In this state, there are no desires, no images and not even a tinge of expectation. Only by practicing this "Wholeness" can we write pages of happiness in each individual's Book of Life.

The mind of the ordinary human being – based on the "ego" – runs like a ghost, either towards the past or towards the future. It is always frightened of the present, because the Reality of the moment dissipates its fragmented energies, trapped in the dimension of time.

By using Light-Attention as an instrument as we encounter the conditioned mind, it disappears instantly, without leaving any residues. Simultaneously with its disappearance, our being is integrated into Reality and we truly and fully live the Absolute Truth.

Spiritual Powers

Spectacular abilities which nourish and define the "self",
They exist in every human being – in an active or latent
form.
Astral journeying, walking on water or on embers,
Clairsentience and astral visions, even bringing the dead
back to life.
The list of real powers that lie within us is infinite.

On the path of ascension, they are often a burden,
They are chains that bind us, with profound negative
consequences;
Because we love them so much – they enhance the "ego",
They degrade and chain us, instead of liberating.

In their essence, powers are neither good nor bad,
The importance we give them creates a prison.
If we see them as relative, we realize their real value,
Through understanding – as useful in certain
circumstances
To those who are in need of healing
Or as simple information, on the path of "Self-knowing".

In each human being, on a psychological level, certain paranormal or parapsychological abilities exist in a latent form. To name a few: astral clairvoyance and clairaudience, reading thoughts, levitation, healing without medicines, astral journeying, stigmata etc.

These traits can become manifest spontaneously, or as a result of certain practices based on will, effort and imagination. Out of ignorance or misunderstanding, some people erroneously consider these phenomena as undeniable signs of spiritual evolution. The phenomenon in itself can morally degrade the individual, when it is followed by vanity, arrogance, self-importance and pride. All these add to the pseudo-values already existent within the structure of the "ego".

In fact, powers are neither good nor bad. The importance we give them can be truly detrimental. We must never desire them. If they reveal themselves, by themselves, we need to give them only the relative importance they deserve by definition.

This title is a warning to all individuals in which such a power has become manifest. But it is equally revealing to the rest of their fellow beings who see an obvious sign of divinity in that particular individual. Do not fall into such a trap!

History is full of examples of ordinary human beings who have been considered and declared to be saints on the basis of such paranormal powers. From the same historical past, we learn that such characteristics have been deemed as diabolical by organized religions, and many unfortunate souls have ended their life on the flames of the pyre.

In conclusion, whoever is endowed with such a trait must never give it any spiritual importance. That person needs to use it in order to help his fellow beings, without turning it into a means of material profit. Using these abilities with love, in the true interest of human beings, will provide far greater advantages on the always ascending path of spiritual evolution.

I See Pure Consciousness in Everything and Everywhere

The Universe – without center, boundless – infinite
existence,
Impossible to encompass with the limited mind;
All things which define it – seen or unseen –
Are, in their essence, energy and consciousness.

From rocks to human beings – galaxies, stars, planets –
All are endowed with consciousness;
For energy and consciousness go hand in hand,
They are inseparable, as one.

In the nucleus of the atom and its finer subparticles,
Consciousness is manifest,
Affirming itself as purity, newness each moment,
It is never repetitive – always Reality.

When we watch a rock in the right manner,
An immediate contact – a direct relationship,
The pure Consciousness within us and within the rock
                                        becomes "One",
Their Source is the same, perpetually manifest.

We and all there is are enveloped in this energy,
In fact, only energy exists, in perfect harmony.
All is within her – the external forms differ,
As essence, all is one "Whole" – in our Sacred inner nature.

When we discover this pure Consciousness
                        within ourselves,
Our whole being is transformed – energy is refined;
The "ego" is dissolved, for it is a fictitious structure,
Violent, egocentric, tough, obsessive and possessive.

In this empty space, Love appears spontaneously,
It directs our actions, our being is new;
Compassion is perpetually present – we feel compassion
                                        even for a rock,
We do not hit it, throw it or mistreat it.

There is no separation between us and all there is,
A constant unity, one reality;
The Unnamable, through Love, envelops us,
Both in this world, as well as after death.

Responsibility

We are responsible, in a real way,
For what is happening nowadays in the world:
Confusion and fear, injustice, violence,
Greed, hatred and fierce battles,
Countless desires and passions
Transform life into a cruel inferno;
The master of the Earth is in a constant state of fear.

Whenever you and I think or speak,
We create dishonest deeds,
Whether we want this or not,
Whether we know this or not,
We contribute to the general chaos;
By sharing what we give out,
We create the world's current madness.

It is an ebb and flow, ceaselessly active,
A constant pollution, created by all of us;
We and the rest of the world are a unity,
United as one breath, one reality.
If we understand our connection with the whole,
Even our thoughts influence the world,
We become more aware and the world is reborn

To a new life of peace and joy;
Through us, day by day, moment to moment,
We transform the whole world,
For each impulse of peace, coming from within our being,
Creates harmony, dissipating all the chaos.

Are we in the least preoccupied by the immense moral and spiritual chaos humanity lives in at the moment? Or, living enclosed in our small universe of egoic interest, we either completely ignore anything that is outside our "ego", or we choose the comfortable option of considering ourselves not to be responsible for it!? And one more question: Are we or are we not conscious of the mutual psychic influence between human beings?

In recent years, much has been written about the phonic and chemical pollution of the environment on the physical plane. Rarely someone mentions psychic pollution, usually timidly and with little conviction. This title, as a consequence of "Self-knowing", has been written in order to fill this void.

Each of us has the potential to become either an inexhaustible source of universal harmony or a hotbed of destructive disharmony.

In the first circumstance, we function as an integral being, in permanent, direct contact with the present, moment to moment. In this fortunate case, we move and act detached from the time-space conditioning, under the direct guidance of creative intelligence, directing us through revelatory intuitive impulses. Any life problem we encounter is quickly solved by kindness and Absolute Love, our intrinsic inner qualities.

In union with the reality of life, such a blissful person is a true psychic depolluter. The harmony of his being is like a laser, dissipating all that is relative, chaotic or negative, without leaving any residues. He is like a lightning rod against all the psychic energies; he annihilates the dysfunctional energies of the "ego", spontaneously and effortlessly. He is a driving force, perpetually stimulating progress and spiritual evolution on the ascending spiral to Infinity.

In the second state, as limited beings, slaves of our own possessions, everything we do has a negative influence, both on ourselves and on the surrounding environment. Living at the level of surface consciousness, generated and fueled by the "ego" fiction, we are responsible for the unhappiness which follows us like a shadow. Furthermore, our unhappiness and its intrinsic negative energies pollute the whole environment. Unwillingly and unknowingly, the turmoil of the mind influences the whole world, whether we are aware of this or not.

The traumatic, conflictual energy we give out in the form of thoughts, images, verbal expression or deeds has a real influence on all our fellow beings, who also function at the same egocentric level. Our activity on this level of existence is defined by that which we emanate; what we give out, we will also attract. A negative attitude attracts similar negative energies.

If, somewhere in the world, people deceive, lie to each other, hate or kill one another, we are also responsible for all this, through our similar psychic emanations, originating in the thinking process. Because of ignorance, unconsciousness or superficiality, we become co-authors or accomplices to terrible deeds happening in the world.

The purpose of this title is to bring awareness to the negative influence caused by our psychological structure, as a limited and obsessive "ego". Simply becoming conscious of this dysfunctional way of "being" – with the help of lucid Attention – leads us to the state of psychological emptiness; the Sacred within us showers its beneficial influence. This is the true man, hidden in the depth of our being, and it is our duty to discover him.

Exposing the "Ego"

Constantly expose the limited and small-minded "self",
Show it no mercy! It is never right!
If you see it as it is, if you encounter it with the light of
Attention,
It immediately disappears. In its place, the real man
appears.

Always present, moment to moment – body and mind
as one,
United with Life, the enlightened being
Encounters Love, in a perfect way,
As well as true "goodness" – a simplicity of experience.

In fact, by exposing the "ego", our whole being opens
Through Sacred Purity, we expand into Infinity;
In this stillness, in humble simplicity,
Devoid of stressful thoughts, we are divinity itself.

Being and melting with the Sublime Boundless,
We create a new world, a Paradise on Earth,
Where all of us experience Happiness in a real way –
A natural effect of our holy attainment.

As soon as we realize, through personal discovery, that the "ego" or the "personal self" is our fiercest enemy, obstructing the experience of peace and happiness, we must never allow it to affirm itself in our relationships with our fellow beings and with Life in its daily unfoldment. Any indulgence as far as the "ego" is concerned will result, sooner or later, in sadness, sorrow and suffering.

Therefore, in order to understand Life authentically and directly, we need to have an intransigent attitude; we must not make any compromises with the "ego".

Following this line of moral conduct with persistence and perseverance, each time we will encounter this intruder with the flame of Attention. The simplicity of this meeting with the ego exposes it and dissipates its image. Simultaneously with its demise, our being becomes whole and it expands spontaneously into the Infinite.

In this new state of humble simplicity and perfect stillness, we are Divinity and, by becoming one with the Sublime Limitlessness, we create the foundation for a new world and a new civilization, a true Heaven on this planet.

The happiness to which every human being aspires reveals itself, by itself, spontaneously, to all those who sacrifice their deceitful "ego" or personality, with its vast array of desires, concepts, ideals, faiths, hopes, despair and fears.

Psychological death is the only modality of giving ourselves totally, melting into the Great Love – the Source of the whole of existence from which all originates and to which everything returns, according to the mysterious fulfillment of Eternity. Let us never forget that all-encompassing Attention is the golden key, opening the gate to the Kingdom of Heaven. Therefore, let us use this key as often as possible. Try it!

We and the World are "One"

I am neither time nor space,
I am perfect unity;
Body and mind as one,
Eternal Reality.

I am nameless and formless,
I am here and in the Infinity,
Where eternal Love
Reveals its reality.

All I can encompass
With my silent experience,
I see it exactly as it is,
United in godliness.

We and the World are "One",
An eternal communion;
Our Mother... Holy Immortality
Our Father... Creative Force.

In man lies God – Essence,
With It, we are in everything,
Neither beginning nor end,
Everlasting Eternity.

This is what the Aliveness reveals,
When we look into our depths
With the light-Attention
And eternal freshness.

In this title, we describe the encounter with oneself and with the world in simple words. In fact, all the poems, as well as the prose versions, are in perfect correspondence with the reality of facts.

Truth cannot be found in the diversity of opinions. It has only one facet. Do we truly encounter it or do we merely talk about it? This is the whole problem. When we encounter Truth directly, everyone sees It in the same way.

Let us explain the holy simplicity of the Reality of our being – body, mind and spirit – in perfect union, "here and now", in direct communion with the moment. My mind is constant freshness; it does not travel to the past, or to the future. Moving in the present moment, I melt into Eternity. I am nameless and formless. I am here and in the Infinite, I am everywhere, manifested as absolute Love. Everything I encounter, I encompass with my silent mind and associate it with God – one Reality, manifesting Its existence. The world and I are a single Unity, in perfect communion. Our mother is immortality and our father is creative force.

That which we call God exists, as Essence, within every human being; we were never separated from It. Why do some of our fellow beings not encounter It and some even deny Its existence? The explanation is simple.

Man, at one point during his long evolution, created the "personal self", by considering himself to be a separate entity from the Great Whole and misinterpreting his existence as a thinking being. In the beginning, he identified with the physical body, then with his increasing intellectual baggage. Because of this error, he created an egocentric culture; its negative effects are too obvious to need mentioning. What we see nowadays in the world is nothing but a natural effect of this past mistake, when the "personal ego" deemed himself to be separate from Divinity.

How can we correct this error? It is very simple! We just listen to and watch ourselves, with the flame of lucid Attention, each time the individual mind reacts to the impressions coming from the external world or from within our being. When we encounter it in this manner, the fiction of the "ego" is dissipated; in the silence that ensues naturally, we discover that we are "One" with Eternity, in a permanent hallowing newness.

Finally, as the vessel of our consciousness becomes empty, we return to the Source of the Sacred, from where we originated once – as absolute Purity, free from the residues of the world and all the vanities we accumulated in association with gross matter.

Religion

A collection of rituals of imaginary values,
Worthless, meaningless ideals;
Words are being uttered, about God, Love;
They are but a product of thinking.

Advice on life is given, as well as reassurance after death,
An arrogant tactic, pretending we are being taken care of.
Just empty promises, all is deceit,
It provides a desperate world with an imaginary support.

There is nothing holy in forms, ceremonies, practices,
Colorful appearance with no substance;
It feeds the ignorance of desperate human beings,
It offers them cheap hope, that they are being protected.

Real religion has no rituals and no formulas,
It has no purpose, no limits;
Living in the present, a state of harmony and
                                active peace,
An integrated human being, overwhelmed with joy.

Thinking cannot comprehend it, it is not a prisoner of the
"ego",
The whole being expands, overcoming limitations.
Religion is the path of freedom, detached from the past,
In a climate of fullness, the individual is eternally reborn.

Religion is perpetual love, constantly renewing itself,
A constant attention, hallowing any human being.
Real religion is the religion of silence,
Through it, in humbleness, we discover the path of
integration.

In the beginning of his existence as a rational and sociable human being, our distant ancestor lived in direct, immediate contact with the present. In perfect union with the mobility of life, in the moment, his whole activity was directed intelligently by the Sacred within through revelatory intuitions. His vital necessities were instantly resolved in the most useful manner.

With the help of lucid, clear attention, accompanying him at all times, he was in constant communion with the Great Cosmic Energy, a natural fulfillment of the religious phenomenon. This direct connection with God represented, therefore, the practice of true religion.

Within this psychological structure, he had a pure consciousness, manifesting itself as Love, beauty and kindness, creating a state of true happiness. Any psychological imaginary anticipation, any purpose or goal as a projection into the future, were completely absent, as the "ego" fiction had not appeared yet. Innocence and humbleness accompanied all his actions, allowing everything to happen without any need for effort or will. Dual options were, in this circumstance, completely foreign to him.

It is difficult to say how long this state of paradise lasted. We can nevertheless assume that temptations started appearing on both planes: the inner world of sensations, as well as the external world, his fellow beings and the surrounding environment.

Of course, it was not easy to be content with simply living the moment, forgetting it without memorizing pleasant or unpleasant experiences; on the basis of these past experiences, he eventually created a scale of moral values, to which he could resort at a later time. I deem that, soon afterwards, the first "self" opinion appeared and, with this unfortunate event, the foundation of the egocentric consciousness was laid.

Therefore, this simple self-image represents the core and the cause of the whole spiritual and moral degradation that followed.

For this reason, the primordial man's state of happiness, in which he was master of everything that existed on Earth, was short-lived.

No one banished him from the Paradise he lived in initially. He did this himself, by renouncing the eternal in exchange for the pseudo-values of this fleeting world. His consciousness as a divine being, which he was aware of in the beginning, was progressively undermined and, finally, completely obscured by the new small-minded egoistic consciousness which became his new identity.

This new identity accompanied him day and night, his whole behavior characterized by confusion, ignorance and fear. From this perspective, life became a burden; he needed to struggle both with his inner reactions, which were more and more difficult to control, as well as with the now-hostile surrounding environment.

Trapped in this psychological structure, he tried to find ways to regain the happiness he had experienced earlier. But no matter how noble and well-meaning the intentions of this confused man were, he could not overcome the limited shell of his conditioning. To put it another way, each activity of the individual as "ego", based on knowledge, can only discover something that is already known or imagined, according to his ideals and personal goals.

Thus, functioning on this level of relative understanding, our ancient ancestor started to create primitive and completely aberrant forms of so-called religion. With the passing of time, these religions evolved, taking more and more subtle forms, filled with secrets and promises, whose practical application does not confirm the desired results.

In the beginning, he worshipped the misunderstood natural phenomena. Lightning, thunder, earthquakes etc. were the first elements which stimulated the fearful man's imagination; he asked for mercy and support from them, in exchange for various sacrifices.

Later on, looking at the sky, he created the cult of the Sun, the Moon and the stars. Further along, looking at the earth, he created the world of gods; he imagined them with the characteristics and weaknesses of human beings. In order for them to be accessible at all times, he captured their appearance in stone, wood or paintings.

From animism to polytheism, religion gradually evolved towards a monotheistic system, recognizing only one divinity. Throughout these attempts to find the Sublime, the world of ideas and images became more complex and diversified. All this informational baggage only enhanced the importance of the "ego", further complicating the understanding of Truth, as well as human interrelations.

In our contemporary world, major religions with their countless sects, as well as the religion of atheism, believing only that which can be perceived by the senses – dead matter as the only reality – do nothing but further fragment and separate the inhabitants of planet Earth.

Each religious system, organized as a hierarchy, firmly states that it is the only one possessing the absolute truth, bringing various arguments in this regard. Therefore, all religions have this categorical pretense that only by following their path will the crowds of believers conquer Eden. All such statements are and will remain unfounded. In practice, they prove to be fruitless, even psycho-somatically detrimental.

On the other hand, what can we say about the religious leaders, who propagate hatred and enmity between human beings, pursuing worldly, petty advantages? Unfortunately, history provides countless examples in this regard, reprehensible deeds with unfortunate consequences.

Killing in the name of God, with the blessing and encouragement of the priest; this fact speaks for itself, proving the insanity of the so-called religious man! What could we say about religious wars or the period of inquisition?!

By mentioning these examples, my only intention is to remind us of the historical past of this world. The saddest thing is that we do not learn anything from the mistakes made by our ancestors!

Unfortunately, even in present times we can witness the same bloody conflicts and confrontations with religious motivations as the ones that occurred in the past. The same fanaticism and personal agendas shed innocent blood, convinced they are fulfilling the divine will.

Faced with these truths, easy to verify by anyone, we ask

ourselves the following question: Is there any way to redeem – spiritually and morally – the individual who lost the initial connection with God?

Before answering, let us see what are the obstacles preventing this communion. Certainly, the main impediment is our egocentric way of functioning; in its arrogance, the "ego" attempts to lead us to the ideals of the Sacred. But the "ego" is modeled according to the religion we have inherited from society. We have accumulated lots of information about God from this environment. For instance: that He is kind, forgiving, that He helps us and rewards us for our good deeds, but He also punishes us if we transgress certain laws etc.

The biggest mistake religions make is that, instead of elevating the individual to that state of humble purity and, through it, to comprehend, from personal experience, what is God, Truth, Reality, Love – they brought Boundlessness down to the level of the limited human mind. As a consequence, each individual created a personal god, different from that of his fellow beings.

If we truly met God even once, we would not be able to use Him as a source of contradictions and conflicts.

If God, this Holy Energy, is everywhere and in everything, as all religions state, in that case He is also within all of us, without any exception. As He is very close to us, in the depth of our being, let us discover Him, right here, right now.

How can we do this? Through the activity of the mind, using images, invocations or repeating formulas? By giving Him gifts and sacrifices or by torturing ourselves in order to impress Him and attract His pity? The list is endless...

Practically, this is what all religious believers are doing, hoping to get what they want, both in this life as well as in the afterlife, the Kingdom of Heaven, as a reward for their effort and struggle.

None of these activities can lead us to the encounter with God or to the eternal happiness we desire to attain. The reason is very simple and logical – rationally, morally and spiritually. Each search for "That which is boundless", performed by the "ego" or the "self" pursuing a goal and functioning egocentrically, is nothing but an obvious arrogance and impiety. In the limitedness of our mind, no matter how cultured it may be, it is impossible to encompass and comprehend the endless ocean of the Cosmic Energy.

The moment we discover this simple truth – that our mind is unable to encounter and understand the Unknown – the surprise of its inability makes it become silent. In the psychological void ensuing naturally, the Divine Spark from the depth of our being reveals itself in all its boundless authority and holiness. This is, in fact, the true, real man, manifested as a state of pure consciousness, beyond space and time, functioning in direct communion with the Infinite.

This blissful moment unites us psychologically and somatically, creating a perfectly harmonious unity in which Love, beauty and goodness transform our whole mentality and behavior. This phenomenon can also be defined as a state of transcendence of the "self", union with the Great Whole and integration into Infinity.

It is only in such moments of peace, silence, equilibrium and inner harmony that radical beneficial transformations take place in the psychological structure of the individual.

In conclusion, the humble silence of the activity of the mind is the only modality to fulfill true religion. Silence is the prayer opening the path to the Sacred, uniting us with Eternity. Lucid attention is the only instrument we use in order to encounter this void or emptiness of thinking.

Who Am I Truly?

Am I the science or the wealth, creating my identity?
Am I the fame, glory, power I am attached to?
Am I the faith or ideal that I bow to,
And arrogantly, I imagine that I know God himself?

All are dreams, fictions. I am none of these!
When all these are illuminated, I see their hollowness,
They are immediately dissipated; in the "emptiness",
                                        Love appears,
I am extended into Infinity – a creative being.

This is the true, real man – always present within me,
Inviting me to discover him, through the right action;
Attention is the path – the instrument which demolishes
The chaotic "ego" – a deceptive structure.

Psychologically – I am "Nothing" – the whole being is
                                        enlightened,
Without center, without bounds – immaculate Purity.
Melting into Eternity, I watch everything as it comes,
Constant Attention – the divine instrument.

Never, in any circumstance, let yourselves be deceived by what you know or by what you own, such as possessions, riches, knowledge, information or experiences. All these possess you and increase your self-importance, strengthening your "personal self". The psychological importance derived from these possessions is always accompanied by sorrow, conflictual states and stress, which tells upon your moral as well as physical health.

Let us ask ourselves the following questions: Are we the knowledge or the riches which create our identity? Are we the fame or glory we are so attached to? Are we the faith or ideal we worship and, in our hideous arrogance, we deem that we have already reached the supreme Truth?

We are none of these; without any exception, they are mere fantasies, a naive child's dream, ephemeral fictions. By encountering them with the flame of Attention, they are spontaneously dissipated, proving they were nothing but frail vanities. Let us see what happens next.

In the "emptiness" or the "psychological void" that ensues intrinsically – as these fictions disappear spontaneously – our being expands into Infinity as a state of Pure Consciousness and Pure Love. This is the real man, functioning as a "Whole", in perfect harmony with that which is real, "here and now". He is Pure Presence, united with Eternity in its endless movement and freshness on moments of existence. Finally, we need to mention that the passiveness of the mind or psychological death detaches the experiencer of "Self-knowing" from his entire past; he becomes a divine instrument, creating a beneficial transformation for the whole of humankind.

Some Live As If in a Dream

From dawn till dusk, some live as if in a dream,
Acting like robots, in what they say, do or think;
The mechanicalness of the mind guides them,
Docile, they listen to it and follow it automatically.

Detached from Reality, they feed on memories,
Facts which occurred once – in the present – empty
                                        deceptions;
Prisoners of the past, they venture into the future
Through hollow imagination – a deceitful support.

What I state here is not a theory! You can discover it for
                                        yourselves,
Watching your thought process, you will find clarity!
Our thoughts are an indication of our moral evolution,
In the depths of our being – lies the best school!

It teaches us about the finite and its empty pettiness,
We are its mere toys, conditioned by the time dimension,
Its whole activity is an egocentric movement,
Creating more sadness in our life.

From the same mysterious school, we discover the Infinite,
When the finite is silent, the Infinite envelops us.
Without any effort or concentration,
Only Attention makes it silent, without any exertion.

We and Boundlessness are "One", as a "Whole" – Divinity,
In this environment we live true moments;
The mind is enlightened, we overcome the worldly,
All dreams are shattered – all within us becomes holy.

Are we aware that our mind functions topsy-turvy, point-lessly?

Can you see how it runs chaotically: either towards the past, or towards the future – uselessly?

If you consider this ceaseless running as something normal, logical and reasonable, you are condemned to stray for the rest of your life!

Why is it that, each day, in our wakeful state, we behave as if in a state of dreamful sleep?

In fact, whether awake or asleep, we are both conscious and unconscious. The cause of this anomaly lies in the mechanicalness of the mind. We have a robotic, unintelligent mind; it unconsciously brings up memories of facts we have experienced in the past – in the present mere dry, dead images – or it projects us into an imaginary and uncertain future. In both cases we are brutally detached from the Reality of Life, we miss Its constant flow and we are unable to perceive Its presence.

Practically, living in the past or in the future is a useless waste of energy. Many accidents at work or car crashes are natural consequences of this lack of attention, caused by the unconscious detachment of our being from the reality of facts and things.

What else do we discover as we inquire into the ceaseless flow of thoughts and feelings appearing on the surface consciousness?

These imaginary apparitions are an indication of our moral and spiritual state of being. All that I state here are not theories, but real facts that you can discover for yourselves. By observing these thoughts attentively, we notice that we are egoistic beings, conditioned by the erroneous education we have received from our family environment, from school, books, disorderly life etc.

If we are able to clearly see this deficiency, are we willing to try a different way of encountering Life?

Here is how we can experience this reality, through "Self-knowing":

Perfectly attentive, we expose the fragments of thoughts, desires or images which attract us into the past or project us into the future. By simply exposing them, they are instantly dissipated; in the ensuing silence, our being becomes whole and, in a state of quietude, we transcend from the finite world of things and phenomena into the Sacred Infinity.

In this dimension we truly experience boundless Love and unconventional Happiness. We and the Sublime Reality are "One", as Divinity. Only in this state can we live moments of true life.

Therefore, when the mind is illuminated with the help of lucid Attention, we leave the climate of worldly preoccupations, and the dreams of the "ego" are shattered – within us, all becomes holy, without any intervention on our part.

Encountering the Boundless

It is impossible to embrace and comprehend the
                                        Infinite Universe
With the limited "ego";
All is experienced in total silence,
Free from time – the being and the mind are newly born.

Thus, I am Immensity, in perpetual movement,
In Unity with the Whole – a creative structure –
I see, feel and act in perfect union with the Sacred,
I use language to describe Wisdom.

One with the Boundless, I am Happiness,
A divine gift, with no support in the thought process;
Happiness has no motives – a supreme satisfaction,
To which, consciously or unconsciously, each human being
                                                  aspires.

The instrument of realization,
An all-embracing, all-encompassing Attention,
In direct contact with Life in its eternal movement;
It is devoid of purpose or ideal formulas.

This simple encounter dissolves the baggage of the mind,
Possessing us with its unintelligent approach.
In the silence that ensues, we are integrated,
                              spontaneously,
We and Boundlessness are "One", as a united "Whole".

The knowing mind of the ordinary man exists as a limited intellect, conditioned subjectively by its memory residues, which separates him from his fellow beings. It functions in a fundamentally egoistic manner, isolating the human being from the surrounding environment.

Each activity initiated and fueled by the mind creates the "ego" or the "personal self" which cannot, in any circumstance, overcome its capacity of understanding conditioned by its time-space perception. Therefore, with this "self" we will never be able to embrace and comprehend the Boundless Infinite, Divinity or Sublime existence, revealing its mysteries by itself on present moments flowing eternally.

The Boundless comes from eternity and flows towards eternity as endless newness and freshness on moments of existence. We can only encounter It in the absolute silence of our ordinary mind. The passiveness of the mind is, therefore, the golden key, opening the gates to Infinity. It liberates us from our whole memory content and, as free beings, we are endowed with a new, fresh, pure mind, extended into Infinity, uniting us with the Boundless.

In the unity of our being, we move and act in perfect union with the Sacredness; we will use language with wisdom, only in order to communicate this phenomenon to our fellow human beings. This union also brings us Happiness, as a priceless gift which fulfills our being to such an extent that nothing else is needed.

In order to realize this communion between "Man and Sublime", we will only use the Light-Attention, which is, in fact, the Sacred itself in action. Therefore, this Attention is not in any way connected to the attention initiated and sustained by the activity of the mind. It is all-encompassing, all-inclusive, and it ensues spontaneously, as a response to the movement of Life.

Using the flash of Attention, we come into direct contact with the reactions of the mind, created by the thinking process as an automatic reaction to the challenges of the Aliveness in its eternal movement. A simple encounter with these reactions makes them disappear and, in the silence that ensues naturally, our being is integrated, united with Boundlessness.

Wisdom

It is here and everywhere,
It has no country and no master,
It was not created by anyone
And no one can create it.

A priceless impulse from eternity,
Vibrating beauty,
A simple harmony
Acting through itself.

What is crooked becomes straight,
What is scarce becomes plentiful,
It shares its abundance,
It integrates that which is dispersed.

Traveling day and night,
Its wise action
Is manifested in facts
Based on Truth.

You can call it Godliness,
You can name it Reality,
You can call it Love
Or Immensity.

The moment you name it,
In thought or speech,
If you define it in words,
It disappears in a flash.

The limited entity,
Trapped in time,
Lives in bondage
And is blinded by deceit.

When the limited is silent,
The whole being expands,
Within us, everything is transformed,
Eternity envelops us.

One with Boundlessness,
Our being is Wise,
A natural fulfillment,
A complete integration.

The word "Wisdom" expresses that supernatural force which the human mind, throughout the millennia, has also called Truth, God, Cosmic Energy, Infinity.

Because of the utmost importance of this topic, I will try to describe it in detail, in order to facilitate a better understanding of the subject.

Certain philosophers or religions claim that, in the beginning, man lived in direct contact with Truth. He lived in a state of happiness, and the whole of nature, all animate beings, surrendered to him as the only master. An indescribable state of paradise reigned on the entire surface of the Earth, unfolding in perfect harmony. There was no violence. Animals did not devour one another, and the grass of the plains and the roots and fruits of the trees satisfied the needs of all living beings.

After a period of time, man started to transgress the wonderful laws of nature. The consequences of his sin were disastrous. Harmony disappeared. The whole of nature was in a state of unbalance and man suddenly found himself surrounded by a hostile environment.

Other theoreticians affirm that man made a qualitative leap, from an inferior level of evolution to a superior one. As a consequence of the natural process of evolution, he started to become more aware of the uncertainty of life. In order to find peace, he began to look for something beyond, for some form of certainty, calling it by different names and endowing it with divine characteristics.

It is not important to us which of these two views is the

true one. One thing is certain: man, frightened by certain natural phenomena that he could not understand with his mind, in fear of wild animals, superior to him in strength and cunning, started to look for a more powerful entity which could provide him with comfort, help and security.

From the very first steps in this direction, man unfortunately made two grave errors. The first is that he used imagination as an instrument of investigation and the second is that he searched for this divine power outside himself. These capital errors have been maintained throughout the whole history, preventing him from discovering the Truth.

Looking at the sky, he imagined a God living in the Sun or the Moon. Glancing at the earth, he deified different insects and animals or created idols with human characteristics. The ancient Romans had over ten thousand gods.

With the invention of the first god, the foundation of religion was laid, with its whole range of dogmas, ceremonies and rituals. In order to honor or tame the gods, the most beautiful animals or in some cases even human beings were sacrificed on altars; with this act, the priest started to gain importance and authority, as he became the only intermediary between men and gods; in some cases, he was even deemed as divinity.

As time passed, religions evolved; they moved from idolatry to theism (monotheism and polytheism). They differed only in their forms of expression and the particular manner of making sacrifices – whereas their idea of God was very similar.

In idolatry, as well as in theism, we encounter the same belief in a superior being, which our ancestors imagined as a statue endowed with divine powers. In both cases, Truth continued to remain a mystery, even up to the present day. In order to find undeniable proof for these statements, it is sufficient to look at the map of the world and its different religions.

The major religions, the hundreds of different sects, various disciplines, methods or philosophies, each with its own relative outlook on life, only chain and separate human beings; they represent the most obvious proof that humanity has not yet discovered the Absolute Truth.

Of course, during this long period of time, certain individuals who attained this wondrous discovery, through a real experience – true titans of spirituality – have always existed. Each time, they were misunderstood both by their contemporaries as well as by their descendants.

Completely misunderstanding their message, generally, people turned these blissful experiencers of truth into spiritual models and authorities, and they worshipped them. The Truth remained, nevertheless, a mystery, impossible to grasp.

There is no path that can lead us to the Truth, because such a path implies a static beginning and an end. But Truth is beyond any rules or forms. On the contrary, it is eternal movement and newness, moment by moment.

We cannot approach it or discover it with the thinking mind, because thinking belongs to the limited, whereas Truth is unlimited, therefore, beyond the comprehension of the human mind.

The Truth is not "something" we can search for and eventually find, because It is and will always be the "Unknown" and, as such, It manifests itself each time as newness, seen for the very first time. In fact, we can only search for what we already know. Therefore, any search implies prior knowledge; otherwise, we might encounter it and, without recognizing it, we might just walk on, unaware of Its presence.

If someone assures us they can lead us to Truth, that

person is nothing but an imposter, who has not discovered Truth himself. Such pretense is absurd, and it reflects, beyond any doubt, the ignorance of the person who makes such a statement.

The wondrous discovery of the absolute Truth is the personal realization of each human being. No one can discover it for us; only we can do this.

If this is the case, let us try together, but each for himself, to make this personal investigation. But in order to truly set out on this inquiry, we must discard, from the very beginning, all theories, methods, faiths we have accumulated in time, which condition our mentality. All these, as well as any memory baggage, are an obstacle to this investigation.

Do not approve, nor reject, what I am describing! In this moment, I am nothing but an indicator sign at a cross-roads, inviting you to look in a certain direction. The indicator is unimportant; so is the person describing all this. By watching, you will discover for yourselves the value of these facts. That's all there is to it.

Living in the Truth is, in reality, a state of "being". Our whole being is a complete "Whole", in perfect union with "what is" or "what exists" in that fraction of a second.

Therefore, I am asking you to try – just as I am doing in this very moment – to watch the activity of your thought process. Watching, with the help of all-encompassing Attention, becomes a luminous flash of light; without any comments and without expecting any results, thinking becomes instantly and unconditionally silent. In that very moment, the state of equilibrium, harmony, peace or absolute void ensues effortlessly.

From now on, the "ego" is completely dissolved. We are a true "psychological nothingness"; we have no expecta-tions, without, however, disappearing into nihility.

Practically, we become a state of lucidity or pure consciousness. That and nothing else.

The moment the psychological "ego" disappears, the whole being is absorbed into the immensity of the Cosmic Energy from where it originated and from which it has never been separated. The structure of the peripheral self – a creation of time, based on ignorance and fear – was the only obstacle preventing us from being conscious of Its reality.

This state of melting into the "Whole" cannot be attained through desire, imagination or as a result of expectation. It reveals itself, by itself, in the holy simplicity of the encounter.

In this circumstance, our true being is revealed, as an electron, a state of pure consciousness enveloped in the immensity of the ocean of cosmic energy, in a perfect union. It is only in this state of boundless existence that the human being is Truth, Immensity, Wisdom. It is an extraordinary, timeless direct experience; filled with an indescribable joy. Words are and will always remain powerless, unable to express something from the dimension of Boundlessness. Nevertheless, we use them, lacking any other means of describing and communicating the experience.

As soon as thinking intervenes, everything we have accomplished spontaneously disappears just as spontaneously. Greedy thinking immediately tries to grasp the vague state, a mere echo of the experience of joy which enveloped our being, and tries to explain it.

When we speak about that indescribable "something", it ceases to exist, for the Truth in its eternal movement disappears as the ephemeral moment fades away. A new state of silence will lead to a new melting into Reality, similar to the last encounter, yet a different experience. The newness of the moment is in perfect syntony with this act of living, unfolding endlessly.

There is nothing mystical in this shattering of the personality, followed by the melting into Infinity. There is nothing extraordinary, only an integral union of the human being, performed in simplicity, when the thinking activity completely ceases to exist, as it has understood its powerlessness.

This state can be attained by any human being, regardless of their level of evolution or the surrounding environment, whether one lives in a secluded place or in the midst of a crowd. It all depends on the simplicity of this encounter with ourselves, without making any assessments or comments. The divine Spark, existent in each of us, guarantees the reality of this experience, without any exception. Lucid, all-encompassing Attention is the instrument through which it reveals itself, illuminating and dissipating the chaotic, interfering reactions of the "ego".

When someone reaches this stage of existence, in a perpetual transformation, any other practices he might have followed previously completely and effortlessly detach from him and vanish. They will fall off by themselves, without any intervention from the experiencer.

Although detached from the conditioning of the past, he will never condemn those who are still trapped and ruled by it.

Only by reaching this stage will human beings attain true comprehension. Only by functioning on this level of consciousness will a true perfect union between human beings be realized; all contradictions and differences of opinion will disappear, as they all have their roots in the dimension of the "ego".

Let us end by reminding that no altars can be built for Truth. Dogmas, ceremonies and rituals are meaningless.

Similarly, there is no place for spiritual leaders, for within each human being there is the student (the ego) and the master or teacher (the Divine Spark). When the "ego" is silent, the Sacred Itself envelops us in Its Wisdom. That and nothing else.

About the Author

Ilie Cioara was an enlightened mystic who lived in Bucharest, Eastern Europe. His writings in 16 books describe the experience of meditation and enlightenment, as well as the practice of Self-knowing using all-encompassing Attention. Like Ramana Maharshi, Krishnamurti, Eckhart Tolle, his is a simple message of discovering our inner divine nature through the silence of the mind.

The author's description of enlightenment, in his own words:

I was 55 years old. One morning, waking up from my sleep, I noticed that, psychologically, I was functioning differently from the night before. The mind had lost its usual turmoil. In a state of serenity I had never felt before, I was functioning in perfect communion with my whole somatic structure.

Only after a couple of hours I realized what had happened to me, without pursuing this "something" as an ideal to accomplish. I was, to use a simile, in the situation of a man blind from birth, who had just gained his sight after undergoing surgery. Everything around me was as new. I had an overall perspective on things. A silent mind allows the senses to perceive things as they are.

The mind in its totality had become, through silence, an immense mirror in which the outside world was reflected. And the world I was perceiving directly through my senses revealed its own reality to me. My fellow beings, close friends or complete strangers, were being regarded indiscriminately, with a feeling of love I had never felt before.

If any reaction of the mind surfaced, it disappeared immediately in contact with the sparkle of impersonal Attention. A state of quiet and all-encompassing joy characterized me in all circumstances, whether pleasant or painful. My behavior was that of a simple witness, perfectly aware of what was happening around me, without affecting my all-encompassing state of peace.

The State of the Sublime is, of course, difficult to describe, but not impossible to experience by someone who authentically practices awareness. In order to communicate it, a simple and direct language is used, which is not filtered through reason, because the "ego", with its subjective perception, is no longer there. To put it this way: the psychological emptiness is the one who lives in the present moment, expresses this encounter into words and still remains present and available to the next moment.

Also Available

Ilie Cioara

The Silence of the Mind

Coming Soon

Ilie Cioara

Life is Eternal Newness

and

I Am Boundlessness

Published by O-Books
www.o-books.com

BOOKS

MySpiritRadio